Narrative Writing with Latinx Teens

Narrative Writing with Latinx Teens

Testimonios, Texts, and Teaching

Carla España

Routledge
Taylor & Francis Group
NEW YORK AND LONDON
A Stenhouse Book

Designed cover image: Camila Leiva and Samantha Williams

First published 2025
by Routledge
605 Third Avenue, New York, NY 10158

and by Routledge
4 Park Square, Milton Park, Abingdon, Oxon, OX14 4RN

Routledge is an imprint of the Taylor & Francis Group, an informa business

Credits:
Figure 1.1, Making the Impossible Possible poster (photograph by The Reverend Baba Carlos Alejandro, Brooklyn College Student Activist 1974–1978). Used by permission of the Alliance for Puerto Rican Education and Empowerment (APREE).

Cover in Chapter 2, Lesson 3 and Appendix B from *En Comunidad: Lessons for Centering the Voices and Experiences of Bilingual Latinx Students* by Carla España and Luz Yadira Herrera. Used by permission of Heinemann, a division of Houghton Mifflin Harcourt.

"Metí la pata" poetry excerpt in Chapter 3, Lesson 3 from *Iveliz lo explica todo* © 2023 by Andrea Beatriz Arango. Reproduced by permission of the publisher, Penguin Random House, New York, NY.

ISBN: 9781032754024 (pbk)
ISBN: 9781003473848 (ebk)

DOI: 10.4324/9781003473848

Typeset in Quinn Text
by Newgen Publishing UK

To the Latine authors writing for our young people and the teachers sharing our stories.

Contents

Foreword

What you'll find inside the pages of *Narrative Writing with Latinx Teens* is an extraordinary tool—a revolutionary model of reaching Latinx students' multiple intelligences—celebrating the many sources of wisdom that are both innate and also part of the complex intersectional realities in Latinx identities and experiences. We do, in fact, contain multitudes. In this impactful book, trusted thought leader, Dra. Carla España, introduces a heart-centered pedagogical model that encourages teachers and students alike to lean into the practice of writing: writing as a tool for critical, cultural, and personal liberation.

Though the focus here is on generating writing with students, Dra. España uses critical and emotional readings of carefully and intentionally curated mentor texts by Latinx creatives as the seed from which the writing will grow. It is after all through recognition, the moment one sees themselves reflected in a glimmer of light in a story or poem, the right words in the perfect mishmash of Spanglish, or when one sees others they know and love come to life on the page, that breakthroughs are reached, doors are opened, and students come in.

As I read, I couldn't help but repeatedly ask myself, "What would I, as a native Spanish-speaking immigrant, working poor, middle child of seven, have done if I had been nurtured in my education in this way? What would I, as a poet, have done if I had been given poetry, by Latine writers no less, as an avenue for my evolution much earlier than when I found it?"

In *Narrative Writing with Latinx Teens: Testimonios, Texts, and Teaching,* you'll find a wide range of examples and opportunities to explore how your pedagogical practice can be enriched: how you can reach your Latine students not only intellectually but through heart, through self-reflection, and through mutual understanding if not empathy and compassion. This book presents specific strategies to help you to lead teens through difficult life experiences while, at the same time, show how they might rise above them and create new understandings.

When I was a teenager, my older teenage sister passed away unexpectedly, and it was poetry that saved me. Writing poetry was where I learned to unravel the enormous grief I felt but also where I learned to make sense of the world around me. Thirty-five years later, I've come to understand that writing from the wound first is a necessary, liberatory act. Releasing these wounds onto the page gives me room to be expansive, to not let the wounds confine me but to set myself free to create other work as well. I was so impressed and relieved to find how Dra. España gets to the core of so many issues plaguing our Latinx communities but also sees past these dynamics and makes us fuller, richer because of and in spite of who we are and what we experience.

I am a perpetual learner, and as I eagerly tried the exercises offered in this book, a few incomplete poems emerged, and the discussions sparked ideas for new works I might explore in my writing. It was so much fun to practice being a student again, imagining that any of the educators featured in this book, including Dr. España, were my teacher. In this process, I healed a part of the poverty of my education, a part of my young self who needed the practices offered inside this book so much. And now you, reader, through Dra. España's work, have these intellectual and emotional offerings to make connections with your Latine students, and perhaps reach and heal yourself.

Pa'lante con amor,
Aida Salazar
Oakland, CA
July 13, 2024

Acknowledgments

Writing a book while witnessing the censorship of your field of study, your students violently arrested for being in solidarity with oppressed peoples, and the images and sounds of multiple genocides, is heart work. My heart broke and mended multiple times across months. Whenever I'd share that I was working on a poem, narrative, lesson, or gathering testimonios, I'd get the "I don't know how you do it." This is how: by surrounding myself with beautiful people who keep me grounded while supporting my dreams.

Gracias, estudiantes. I am deeply grateful for the students whose words open up our chapters. Those middle-grade writers who welcomed me into their class when I was a budding researcher, to the undergraduate students who bare their souls as they navigate life on our college campus. There are also the students who—with their protest signs, flags, and keffiyehs—embodied intersectional solidarity as they chanted in rallies, walked in protests, and spoke up at commencement. Brooklyn College students: Christopher Arias, Melisa Castillo, Edgar Castro, Natalie Díaz, Miguel Figueroa, Denice Ocana, Lexington Rivera, Maricruz Sánchez-Hernández, and Valeria Sanchez-Pinet. Thank you all for helping me grow in my courage.

Gracias, profes. To the teachers in my life that listened to the writer within themselves and within me, it was thrilling to be in your midst. I am so grateful that I've had the opportunity to write with hundreds of teachers across the years: some in writing workshops, others in virtual sessions on *En Comunidad* and *Translanguaging Collections*. Teachers who shared stories and responses to poetry writing prompts. We laughed and cried together. We filled our Zoom chats with recommended books. New York City Public Schools, San Antonio Independent School District, El Paso Independent School District, Austin Independent School District, and pre-service teachers at the Kennesaw State University Latinx Teacher Retreat. To the educators who shared their testimonios in this book: Anel V. Rivera Guerrero, Raúl Vaquero, Coral Zayas, Brendaly Torres, and Enrique Lopez Pino. Thank you for being vulnerable with me.

Gracias, colegas. To the City University of New York–New York State Initiative on Emergent Bilinguals community, who with their gatherings always bring so much joy. Khánh Lê for writing with me (now that this book is done, I can join you for gym classes and not use the gym lobby as writing space only). To the team at the Ethyle R. Wolfe Institute for the Humanities at Brooklyn College: Gaston Alonso and Keanna Benjamin. I learned so much as Faculty Associate this year with you! To the Immigrant Student Success Office at Brooklyn College. You are all connecting communities and transforming lives. I'm thrilled we connected this year. To my Department of Puerto Rican and Latinx Studies at Brooklyn College: you're the best! To my department chair, Alan Aja, who always protects my time, and colegas Mike Mena, Jasmine Mitchell, María Pérez y González, and Carla Santamaría. Thank you for your encouragement and for modeling true cariño in academia.

Gracias, artistas. The artists forming part of the soundtrack to this book: Elyanna, Kehlani, Villano Antillano, Mon Laferte, Lido Pimienta, Ana Tijoux. Thank you for speaking your truth. The artistas featured on the book cover: Camila Leiva and Samantha Williams. They painted the Cosechando Comunidad mural at a community garden in Cerro Navia, located in Santiago, Chile. Thank you for sharing your art, especially with that Chile connection. It means so much to me!

Gracias, journalists, legal scholars and poets. Journalists Bianca Graulau and Maria Hinojosa. Human rights attorney, Noura Erakat. Poets Hala Alyan, Ariana Brown, Safia Elhillo, Alan Pelaez Lopez. Thank you for keeping me informed and accompanying me in my rage and healing.

Gracias, mamá, scholars, authors, and friends. Laura Ascenzi-Moreno, María Cioè-Peña, Cati V. de los Ríos, Tracey T. Flores, Paula Guerra, Luz Yadira Herrera, Jasminne Paulino, Pia Persampieri, Nawal Qarooni, Sanjuana Carrillo Rodríguez. Your work is brilliant. You love deeply. You show me how to be present with myself, family, and my career, and when to take a most needed break. You are all a gift.

Gracias, first readers of this project of my heart. Yvonne de Gaetano for loving this when it was an idea in a book proposal. My City University of New York Faculty Fellowship Publication Program writing group: mentor Ted Ingram, and scholars Gail Buffalo, Inés Corujo-Martín, Pedro De La Cruz, Evelyn Durán-Urrea, and Nicora Placa. Thank you for your thoughtful feedback and for believing in this project. The Fall 2022 Latinx In-Community Retreat for Writers at the Highlights Foundation where I revisited this book idea and the poem "Remember Me." José Alfredo Menjivar Ortéz and R. Joseph Rodríguez, poets and educators, for reading my poems. I saved everyone's feedback and will be returning to it for my next book!

Gracias, Stenhouse Publishers at Routledge/Taylor and Francis book team. To my editor, Terry Thompson. What a lovely process this has been! You listen deeply and ask all the right questions. Every conversation and comment on my chapters has made me a better writer. Thank you, Melanie Moy and the production team for seeing my vision as you seamlessly integrated family pictures, poems, narratives, lessons, text sets, and testimonios.

Gracias, familia. Este libro es posible por todo el apoyo que me brindan al cuidar a la chiquita (siempre está con las pilas cargadas corriendo, jugando, bailando y cantando con ustedes), cocinarme comidas ricas (papá con empanadas Chilenas), y mostrar interés sobre lo que estoy escribiendo. Gracias por creer en mi (mi mamá, tan chistosa preguntándome si mis libros son exitosos como los de la Isabel Allende), y tener todo organizado para crear el tiempo y el espacio para escribir (Angel, siempre estaré agradecida por el calendario en Google y por motivarme a salir sin sentido de culpabilidad cuando tengo que escribir). Mis raíces en Chile con cuentistas en la familia y literatura por toda mi niñez han florecido en este libro. Que dicha poder compartir mi escritura.

En solidaridad,
Carla

Prologue: Escribiendo para desahogarme: Writing as Release, Resistance, and Reimagining

I asked Oscary why she wrote about that particular moment in her life. Oscary said "porque yo quería escribir, desahogarme cómo yo me sentía, cuando yo vine aquí sin mi mamá," "because I wanted to write, to 'desahogarme,' how I felt when I came here without my mom." The use of this word "desahogarme" is powerful to me. The fact that a sixth grader would use this word and in this context is powerful. I have had trouble translating it. I have found people use it to mean: to get something off their chest, to vent, to release something huge that is bottled up.

—Field notes, October 20, 2015

Oscary[1] was one of five middle-grade writers I interviewed in an English as a New Language class in New York City (España, 2017) as part of my first research study—one that I had designed as a doctoral student to explore the impact of a bilingual teacher's writing instruction on Latinx youth. The joy, anticipation, collaboration, and curiosity were all palpable when it was time to take out those writing notebooks. Each time I sat with one of these writers and their teacher, I held back tears. They will forever remain with me. They reminded me of the young people in my sixth- and seventh-grade classrooms and my colleagues at Don Pedro Albizu Campos School in Harlem, New York.

Alejandra Medina, the research site teacher and a Peruvian bilingual educator, not only modeled writing to support her students' writing tasks but as a way of resistance to the narratives present throughout her teacher preparation journey that said that she had to "lose" her "accent" and practice reading out loud so students could understand her. Alejandra read and shared the latest middle-grade literature with her students; wrote multiple drafts of narratives, and informational

1. All research participants' (students and teachers) names are pseudonyms in this book.

and persuasive pieces; and met with families on a regular basis, connecting with them before and after school. As an immigrant and bilingual teacher in a classroom that was designed to be English dominant, Alejandra defied the norms by featuring Spanish regional varieties from Peru in her pieces written in English. The students followed her example, teaching their teacher words in Spanish from different areas in the Dominican Republic and Mexico; they wrote multiple versions of personal narratives, fictional stories, and informational pieces, sometimes translating them or providing words in languages other than English; and they did this with such joy that, on days for peer feedback across the writing process, the classroom sounded like a coffee shop with the flurries of conversations, laughter, and notetaking.

Thanks to a City University of New York–New York State Initiative on Emergent Bilinguals (CUNY-NYSIEB) partnership with her school, Alejandra learned about another way to view language, bilingualism, and multilingualism. By seeing these students' (and her own) language practices as products of one linguistic repertoire instead of distinct languages with artificial borders, Alejandra created a space that embraced the students' entire being. Developing an understanding of the discrimination that marginalized speakers faced also helped Alejandra consider her journey and the language hierarchies that were ever so present in her upbringing, teacher education program, and conversations with colleagues. Why would most students from the Dominican Republic be shamed for speaking Spanish when speakers from other areas didn't face that same treatment? Why was it that her largely gentrifying neighborhood in New York City had middle-class and upper-class white families seeking bilingual education for their children to learn Spanish, but for years, the largely Dominican population at her school (and neighborhood) was pushed to assimilate and transition as quickly as possible to mainstream English classrooms?

That shift in Alejandra's language ideologies radically impacted her view of herself, her students, and language(s) in general, leading to changes in her pedagogy. It is at this point that our paths crossed! This was the year the groundbreaking book *The Translanguaging Classroom: Leveraging Student Bilingualism for Learning* (García et al., 2017) was published, giving all of us in the fields of teacher preparation (in both English Education and Bilingual Education) an entry point into our work! Alejandra had the opportunity to learn from some of the book's authors (Kate Seltzer and Ofelia García) through the CUNY-NYSIEB partnership at her school. In Alejandra's writing community, students read their teacher's writing as well as each other's and used all of the features of their language repertoire to make meaning of the exemplar texts and to create their own.

What did it mean, I wondered, that the students in these writing classes, whose journeys seemed so unique and, simultaneously, so much like my own, all described the act of writing as a way to "desahogarse"? I was five when I left my family in Chile and started attending an English-only school in New York City. Soon after, I attended a Saturday Spanish-language program at La Escuela Argentina. Letter writing in Spanish helped me nurture that connection with the family I wouldn't get to see for another five years and my growing understanding of my identity as a writer. I also wondered how my writer identity would've been strengthened in my elementary years if I had bilingual teachers like Alejandra, who were supported by partnerships like CUNY-NYSIEB.

In my interviews with Alejandra's students, after reviewing the writing portfolio pieces where they walked me through their process, I asked each student to share advice they'd give to a newcomer student joining their writing class. One particular writer, Genesis, responded:

> Que no se preocupe. Que si es algo que él, que esa persona está escribiendo muy personal, que él nunca había compartido con alguien que no se preocupe porque si él tiene a Ms. Medina o a usted, él se lo puede compartir para usted para sentirse desahogado y poder escribir. Que si él no puede escribir, si esa persona se siente que no puede escribirla que lo comparta con usted o con Ms. Medina para que se sienta más libre y pueda compartirlo con todo el mundo ... No te quedes callado porque te vas a sentir como más atascado y nunca vas a compartir eso. Te vas a sentir como ahogado.
>
> (España, 2017, p. 163)

Genesis deeply understood the transformative power of writing in this classroom, which was a liberating experience. If you don't open up through your writing, you can do so with the teachers, shared Genesis. "Don't hold it in because you will feel more stuck and you'll never share it. You'll feel as if you are drowning" (España, 2017). I was struck by this sixth-grade writer's advice because most of my school visits to writing classrooms around the country in my capacity as a literacy consultant revealed students who more often described writing as a tedious task and not a liberating one. I wondered what it was about the writing experience in this particular writing community that created space for writing as catharsis. The "undrowning" if you will. A release writers feel when they've been holding back for so long and feel like they can share it all, "I can finally desahogarme," or find release and stop drowning.

As I began to process this thought, I was coming close to a decade as an educator, close to ten years of writing with young people and sharing my writing, first with sixth graders and then with children from all grades on school visits to support with literacy instruction and curriculum development. I knew exactly what Oscary, Genesis, and the other children felt. In moments where it seemed I could no longer hold it all in, it was the page that welcomed me; it was a writing community that listened, read, gave feedback, and showed me that my voice mattered; and it was those thoughtful teachers, like Alejandra, who encouraged me to keep writing and were vulnerable with me as they shared their lives on the page.

Those writers in Alejandra's class thrived because of their freedom to write fully, including their bilingual and multilingual identity. Their Dominican or Mexican words weren't disregarded or shamed by the teacher. Instead, she had come to embrace Latinx students' translanguaging (García et al., 2017; García & Leiva, 2014).

I dream of this for all Latinx teens, especially those employing varieties of Spanish and Indigenous languages that have been delegitimized or deemed "incorrect" as they defy the norms of standardized dominant monolingual Spanish and English languages.

Stories are powerful. Expressing our full selves through narratives and poetry creates and nurtures communities of learners even through difficult moments, and we need to write ourselves into the narrative so much more in these times. Writing for release, resistance, and reimagining engages our entire being. *Narrative Writing with Latinx Teens* is a tapestry of my childhood, adolescence, teachable moments, research, and writing strategies that center varied Latine experiences and translanguaging pedagogy. I hope that teachers' and students' writing lives are nurtured with this book. Thank you for joining me on this writing, healing, learning, and teaching journey.

Chapter One

My Introduction to Writing with Latinx Teens

"Si esa persona se siente que no puede escribirla que lo comparta con usted o con Ms. Medina para que se sienta más libre y pueda compartirlo con todo el mundo ...

No puedes tener miedo a compartir algo bueno o algo malo porque si es algo malo que nunca has compartido, desahógate. No te quedes callado porque te vas a sentir como más atascado y nunca vas a compartir eso."

—Genesis, sixth-grade student (España, 2017, p. 163)

"Don't stay quiet because you'll feel more stuck and you'll never share it," are the words Genesis used as she considered the advice she would give a newcomer student writer in her class (España, 2017). This is a practice I had to cultivate for years as a bilingual writing teacher. Almost a decade earlier, it was Puerto Rican educator and now one of my lifelong mentors, Profesora Yvonne de Gaetano, who told me to keep a journal to write those stand-out moments from my interactions with students. Some of my entries in that first journal I kept as a teacher included Yuleika's "solidaridad" when calling for community solidarity and Sebastián's "es una injusticia" when we were learning about Columbia University's plans for expansion into their neighborhood.

I first had the opportunity to put this sage advice into practice alongside my students like Yuleika and Sebastián at Don Pedro Albizu Campos School, a K-8 public school in Harlem, NY. My school administration and literacy coach supported me with professional learning opportunities and teaching demonstrations. Mentors and colleagues listened to my concerns when curricula, workshops, and methods were monolingual, and we strategized how to modify plans to center what we knew about our students and pedagogy. Teaching writing became one of my favorite times of the school day because I got to know my students and witnessed their joy and process, from drafts to publishing to writing celebrations, with some delicious meals that families from the Dominican Republic, Puerto Rico, Mexico, Peru, and Honduras contributed to our gatherings!

Despite such validating early experiences, I had mixed emotions when I was first given a writing curriculum to teach sixth graders. I had recently finished a graduate degree in Religion and Society, and the New York City Teaching Fellows teaching-preparation workshops before our first year of teaching did not delve into curriculum design but focused on classroom management. My new role as a bilingual sixth-grade teacher was a long way from the letters I'd write to my family in Chile, the papers on books I was assigned to write in high school English classes and the writing tasks from my undergraduate studies. In other words, I was grateful for some direction. My school sent me to a writing institute for writing teachers facilitated by the Teachers College Reading and Writing Project (TCRWP)—now Advancing Literacy within Teachers College Continuing Professional Studies—that first summer before I started teaching my new class. It took a great weight off my shoulders to have a writing curriculum with a scope for the school year, lessons, and sample pieces. This was a helpful way to ease my transition to teaching because I was also busy planning lessons for five different subjects (reading, writing, social studies, math, and science) for my bilingual Spanish-English classroom!

At the same time, after attending a writing institute and making my way as a new teacher through a middle-grade writing curriculum, something didn't sit right with me as I considered my own and my students' experiences, identities, and language practices. Here I was, a Spanish-English bilingual teacher from Chile, teaching in Harlem with bilingual students from many areas of the Latinx diaspora. Although my school's literacy coach and principal never required us to read from the sample lessons in the curriculum, I often felt like I was scrambling to find other texts that better represented our experiences, interests, languages, and storytelling processes. Something was missing.

Thanks to the initiative and brilliance of the administration, literacy coach, and librarian/grant writer that I had at the time at Don Pedro Albizu Campos School in Harlem, I had access to many books and resources to help me with this new learning curve. I began to search my classroom library, mining it for books by Latinx authors, and attended all the local events on Latinx children's books to learn more about an area missing from my schooling. For my first assignment in a literacy course in my teacher preparation program (the summer before I started teaching bilingual sixth graders), I remember selecting the book *The Color of My Words* (*El color de mis palabras*) by Trinidadian author, Lynn Joseph (2001) as I was searching for a book by a Caribbean author and/or with a protagonist from the Dominican Republic. I knew the demographics and neighborhood of the school that hired me, so I wanted to prepare with a middle-grade book that would ignite interest in our reading discussions and narrative writing.

Eventually, with the help of that team at my first school, *El color de mis palabras* and several other books with Latinx protagonists gave way to an emerging, diverse classroom library! Books by Latinx authors helped me and my students feel less alone in our writing. We connected, questioned the roots of the challenges we faced, and better understood experiences outside of our own, given the complexities of the Latinx diaspora. This meant revisiting and reimagining the rubrics, demonstration writing examples, and checklists in the writing curriculum that did not reflect our ways of storytelling. My students were writers navigating multiple languages to craft narratives, and this reality needed to be more prominent in the curriculum.

Translanguaging as a Teacher, Writer, and Researcher

As Sonja Cherry-Paul (2024) reminds us and the founders of the #DisruptTexts movement state in their keynote, "Dismantling and Reimagining the Literary Canon" (The Educator Collaborative, 2020), booklists aren't enough. If we are truly about culturally and linguistically responsive teaching (Paris & Alim, 2017), then we must be intentional about our text selection and instructional use. With encouragement from Dr. Yvonne de Gaetano, I took my concerns about bilingual education in schools with a monolingual curriculum and my love of writing to the Urban Education doctoral program at the Graduate Center, City University of New York. Through our work together—reading through my papers and processing my questions—Dr. de Gaetano connected me to another scholar, Dr. Ofelia García.

Dr. Ofelia García exposed me to translanguaging as theory and pedagogy, naming what I had experienced as a Chilean in New York and as a bilingual teacher. Translanguaging, as an orientation to language that looks at how bilinguals use their full language repertoire (García, 2009), was a new term to me for something I was familiar with, from childhood family moments, teen years as an interpreter for a bilingual Dominican church in Washington Heights, and now my adult teaching life. I appreciated learning that the methods I used to teach my bilingual students could be described as translanguaging pedagogy (García et al., 2017), acknowledging how we navigate our language practices depending on the context, both within literature and in our lives. It was all coming together as I rushed from Don Pedro Albizu Campos on the 1 train to the Graduate Center in midtown to make it to my evening classes. On those commutes, I gathered my thoughts on the read-alouds I did that week and how our reading was informing our writing. Walking past the crowds of tourists on 34th Street to my classes, I wondered, "How can my teaching and text selections better inspire the writers in my class?" and "Could our writing units better reflect the language practices and repertoires I heard and read from my students and their families, or would we forever have to confine ourselves to the limitations of the curriculum written from a monolingual, English lens?" In other words, how could writing for my Latinx students feel the way it felt for Genesis so that they are not "atascados," or feeling stuck in their writing and in their lives?

The seven years I spent in the Urban Education doctoral program at the Graduate Center served as a sounding board and intellectual foundation for these questions and the many others that came up as I left the classroom to pursue literacy coaching with the same organization I had questioned when I began teaching, TCRWP (now Advancing Literacy). At TCRWP, I was learning about literacy curriculum development, albeit through a monolingual English lens. Still, I had opportunities to support teachers' curriculum modification for bilingual/multilingual students throughout the United States and in schools in Chile, Colombia, and Mexico. At the Graduate Center, I was learning how to merge theory and practice with translanguaging as a lens from a bilingual Latina scholar.

When I transitioned into teacher education at Hunter College in their Bilingual Teacher Preparation Program, I focused on how bilingual and multilingual children and their teachers were experiencing schooling. I redoubled my efforts to develop writing spaces that honored and celebrated their lived experiences, and in doing so, I kept returning to these questions:

- Was school a liberating place, or did language-minoritized children and teachers from the global majority feel they couldn't be their whole selves in their teaching and learning spaces?
- What could we do as teacher educators to better support language-minoritized children and pre- and in-service teachers who themselves were racialized bilinguals?
- How could we use our own creative writing and writing instruction to process childhood as writers and educators from the global majority?

I took these questions into my research at a middle-grade English as a New Language classroom in New York City, where I met sixth-grade writers Oscary and Genesis and their bilingual Peruvian teacher, Alejandra Medina. Ms. Medina used writing workshops as a teaching method along with modifications to the sixth-grade personal narrative writing curriculum. In this case study, I observed the class during their personal narrative unit, interviewed the teacher and four students, took field notes on class sessions across the writing process, and analyzed students' narrative writing. What started as an interest in the learning experiences of bilingual students and how their teacher took the monolingual curriculum to make it their own found its footing in the following research questions:

- What language ideologies enable a teacher to modify an existing curricular unit on personal-narrative writing to consider the complex linguistic and cultural practices of emergent bilingual middle schoolers?
- What are the modifications of the curriculum and pedagogy?
- How does bilingual pedagogy help bilingual sixth graders construct written personal narratives that build on their cultural and linguistic resources, and what are its effects?

One of the most memorable classroom moments I observed was when Ms. Medina shared her writing, and then students took their narrative pieces, selected excerpts, and shared them with peers for their feedback sessions. It was authentic, organic, nurturing, and joyful. No "Ugh, we have to write" or "I hate revisions." Instead, the room burst into laughter, and the kids read pieces out loud. Everyone considered themselves writers because the teacher was modeling that example (she had her writing notebook, too), and it was completely normal to write in varieties of Spanish, varieties of English, or both. The teacher's decision to show that in her writing, to have examples of published authors who do the same, and to affirm her bilingual students' pieces that showed these dynamic language practices was one I wished I saw supported in all schools and curricula. I know how transformative writing was for me when I began to write alongside my students, modify curriculum, and design lessons outside of a monolingual scripted curriculum.

It is demeaning to teachers and the profession when we're told to teach the curriculum "as is" or "read from the script." One school leader asked me to do this as a literacy consultant when planning for school visits! This was most egregious when a school or literacy organization leader would advocate for using the scripted curriculum over a teacher sharing their authentic writing. Since this was certainly not my experience at my school, I wondered where the message got lost. Were administrators' and teachers' own raciolinguistic ideologies (Flores & Rosa, 2015) keeping them from affirming the ways of being (including writing) of language-minoritized individuals in their community? In other words, did these institutions trust a curriculum's writing samples more than a teacher's demonstration writing because mostly monolingual, white authors authored them? Was it more acceptable because it was a curriculum with the backing of a large publisher or higher-education institution? Where did culturally sustaining pedagogy (Paris & Alim, 2017) support come in, and if it wasn't in the curriculum development, then where did it exist in the school's professional learning budget and plans?

I've had the opportunity to address these questions on a national level for several years in a community dedicated to teaching English. From the time I taught middle grades through to my graduate and undergraduate teaching, I have been involved in the National Council of Teachers of English, particularly with their Middle Level Section Steering Committee (MLSSC). In that work, I spent four joyful years developing programming that brought together teachers, teacher educators, librarians, authors, and publishers. I learned about the beauty of collaborative planning and the much-needed spaces for teachers to hear from Latinx authors, write their stories, share with others, and be supported in how they plan to bring this all together in their teaching. I remember one particular session where attendees all gave a standing ovation to poet Elizabeth Acevedo as she walked in to celebrate her National Book Award for Young People's Literature for *The Poet X* (2018). My favorite memories are those instances where intimate roundtables of authors and teachers gathered to swap stories and writing strategies. These are the types of memories I hope to replicate for Latinx teen writers.

Ethnic Studies and Teacher Preparation

I continue to explore ways to make this possible. My current role as a faculty member in the Department of Puerto Rican and Latinx Studies at Brooklyn College, CUNY, allows me to teach across an ethnic studies department in the School of Humanities and Social Sciences; and the Childhood, Bilingual and Special Education Department in the School of Education. With over a decade of experience teaching in teacher preparation programs, this role has created opportunities for me to engage with students across different studies. My teaching now more closely brings me to the experiences of our youth as I discuss topics such as schools, youth literature, writing our stories, curriculum, language, and identity.

I don't take any of this lightly, as my freedom to do this is largely due to the Brooklyn College student organizers who were in solidarity decades ago, demanding that their lives be included in the curriculum and teaching faculty (Pérez y González, 2021). The Puerto Rican and Latinx Studies Department (known as Puerto Rican Studies when established in 1970) rose from struggle and community organizing (see Figure 1.1 and Sporn et al., 2021). From protests to sit-ins, student activism was loud, and the administration had no other choice but to listen.

FIGURE 1.1
Making the Impossible Possible: The Story of Puerto Rican Studies in Brooklyn College *poster.*

In her memoir, *Brooklyn Dreams: My life in public education* (2015), Dr. Sonia Nieto, one of the early faculty members and now renowned scholar in bilingual and multicultural education, says this of her time at Brooklyn College: "my political, social, and cultural awareness took a giant leap forward that first year at the college. Although I was hired as an instructor, I was equal parts learner" (2015, p. 150). Now, when I teach ethnic studies and education courses, I take a moment to learn from and honor the shoulders we stand on.

Sometimes, this means that the writing in my "Introduction to Puerto Rican and Latinx Studies" course looks like reflections on documentaries that synthesize social movements in response to educational inequity. In my "Bilingualism in the Twentieth Century" course, students took key quotes from *Brooklyn Dreams: My life in public education* (Nieto, 2015), and shared their personal connections and questions on a digital platform in preparation for Sonia Nieto's conversations with us on her teaching journey. When students read Elisabet Velasquez's *When We Make It: A Nuyorican Novel* (2021) or the Spanish translation, *Y si lo logramos: Una historia nuyorican* (2022), they selected key poems in this novel in verse to reread with their book clubs. They discussed themes related to identity, the Puerto Rican diaspora, gentrification in Brooklyn, family, faith, and machismo. Their writing included poems inspired by Elisabet Velasquez and personal essays on these topics, how they shape their teaching philosophy, and their understanding of how they navigate the world. You can read more of the impact of this book on Latine youth in Brendaly Torres' testimonio (see Chapter 5). My use of youth literature, especially by Latinx authors, is a thread across all of my courses, helping students (most of whom are future educators) process concepts through these texts that serve as additional sources of information (complementing our use of journal articles, books, podcasts, documentaries, and more) and as mentor texts for their writing. Several students leave my courses ready to tell their stories and pursue further lines of questioning related to ethnic studies thanks to our engagement with these texts.

How to Use This Book

This book builds on my years of teaching, coaching, researching, curriculum planning, and writing with teachers like Alejandra from my dissertation research in that English as a New Language classroom; bilingual teachers like my colleagues at Don Pedro Albizu Campos School; in-service teachers taking graduate courses at

LIVING LANGUAGE

Language evolves, and we listen to its users. If I truly believe in creating writing spaces (in my life and in others' lives) that are ways to "desahogarse," as those sixth graders described, then my language also needs to reflect this pursuit. One of the ways we can do that is to heed the words of the queer community in Latin America and elsewhere that call us to do away with the gendered binary in the Spanish language. "Latina/o" does not include everyone, and neither does "Latino" ("Latine" is another preferred term for inclusion that I'm learning to include in my life).

Hunter College; English teachers on my school visits; and our future teachers just starting their journeys in undergraduate ethnic studies and education programs, like my students at Brooklyn College. As for the students in Alejandra's classroom, writing is liberating for me when I can be my full self on the page and across my writing process. This creation of liberating spaces for Latinx teens where they can be themselves fully is why I write and engage in conversations about this matter. It's also why you will not see words in Spanish or Haitian Creole italicized in this book. Haitian Creole and Spanish are not othered; instead, varieties of Spanish are included with varieties of English, allowing me to use my entire language repertoire. This is also why you will see me use inclusive language with the more inclusive term "Latinx" or "Latine" when referring to a group of youth from the diaspora of Latin America.

In grappling with our writing, languages, and identities, I've found it helpful to ground my teaching in my students' authentic experiences, or testimonios, as they speak back to the dominant narratives that dismiss the lives of marginalized people (Figure 1.2). The tradition of testimonios as a research methodology grounded in community comes from Latin America as a way that oppressed communities shared counter-narratives that highlighted their experiences at the intersections of different ways of discrimination and resilience (Huber & Villanueva, 2019). In this book, each chapter is bookended with testimonios; those of my students open the chapter and those of practitioners in the field conclude the chapter. These testimonios help us grow in courage, intellectual curiosity, writing pursuits, and advocacy with and for our students. Maybe on an off moment or day, when you question your path or feel alone in this work, you turn to the testimonios, leaning into the healing that comes from connecting with others' stories. These students

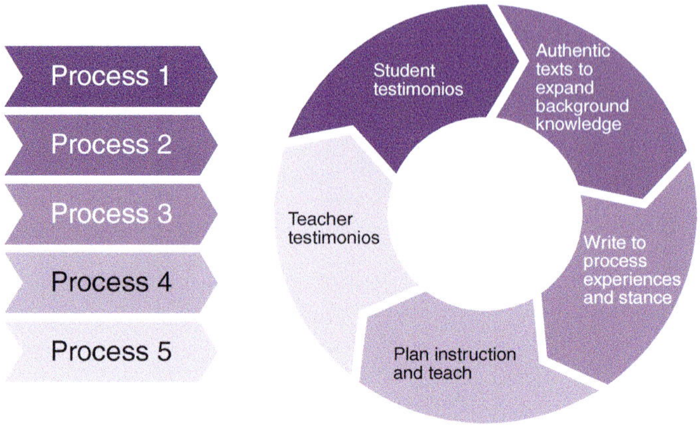

FIGURE 1.2
Writing for Desahogo Teaching Framework.

and educators have nurtured my growth, and I am honored to welcome them into this space and your teaching lives.

As you can see in the Writing for Desahogo Teaching Framework (Figure 1.2), if we are grounded in our students' lives, we can expand our knowledge of the issues that impact them and the ways they are responding and creating counter-narratives (Solorzano & Yosso, 2002) by engaging with more authentic texts on their experiences. We can continue building on that foundation by processing our experiences and stance on these issues through our writing. This is all necessary before we proceed to planning instruction.

To that end, each lesson sequence begins with an introduction to help you expand your understanding of a topic. For some, these topics (migration, mental health, language learning, resilience, communities) reflect and validate personal experiences. For others, these topics and the contents of the mentor texts will be unfamiliar. And still others of us may have briefly considered a topic but only through the dominant narrative lens, reflecting a need to learn the counter-narratives before we delve into curriculum development. For example, after author Julio Anta gave a book talk to middle-grade and high school social studies, bilingual dual language, and English teachers on his graphic novel *Sí, Se Puede: The Latino Heroes Who Changed the United States* (2023), several of them pointed out how they learned more about this history through a handful of pages in that book than from the textbooks of their adolescence, coming to terms with a harsh and bittersweet reality of missed histories in their education while they plan instruction to do better by their students now.

The sample immersion mini-units can be read sequentially or by preference of the current topic of study in the classroom. The mini-units included throughout this book help teachers imagine what instruction can look like when we invite the writers in our class to expand their understanding of content and craft by bringing in multimodal texts, building discussions around them while complementing them with book talks and poems that leave students eager to explore these in their own writing journeys. To that end, each of the following chapters highlights a common theme in the Latinx diaspora—including (im)migration, mental health, language and language learning, resilience, and community—while weaving in:

- Writing pieces
- A lesson sequence
- Suggestions for developing a writer identity and writing life in the classroom
- Teacher text sets for personal study and building background knowledge
- Writing mentor texts for students from poetry, middle-grade fiction, young adult fiction, and memoir
- Teacher testimonios that span from middle grade to high school and higher education to amplify the voices of Latinx practitioners across the United States.

You can access the collection of teacher and student text sets highlighted throughout the lessons at this link.

How might you use this book as an English teacher, writing workshop teacher, curriculum developer, literacy coach, teacher educator, or pre-service or in-service teacher? One way is to use the demonstration writing as a launching pad to nurture your writing life if you haven't tended to this already. Another way is to use the lesson sequences as an entry point for students to familiarize themselves with a topic, texts, and translanguaging (España & Herrera, 2020). These lesson sequences can also help you expand your understanding of bilingualism/multilingualism, translanguaging, and the lives of Latine students learning English while navigating other languages and ways of being. You might dedicate a week at the start of your writing units for this immersion, incorporating the four lessons (multimodal topic launch, poetry, middle-grade fiction, and young adult literature) into the larger scope of your units. I also imagine many of you might return to the included poetry lessons for a stand-alone poetry unit, to celebrate National Poetry Month, or to weave poetry into the fabric of your writing instruction across the school year.

Courage and advocacy go hand in hand as we listen deeply to our students and how they navigate the times they live in. Writing is one of the ways we can process, create, question, and share in community, so like Genesis in that sixth-grade classroom, we feel less alone. We teach and write in a time of rampant censorship; book bans; xenophobia; homophobia; anti-Diversity, Equity, Inclusion and Belonging efforts; and anti-immigrant policies and rhetoric. A time when Latinx families seeking asylum often face separation and dehumanization. We also do this work at a time when some youth are using social media to lift the veil off of propaganda, creating solidarities across oppressed groups, and tracking the effects of colonialism from Puerto Rico to Palestine. A time when adults in teacher preparation programs that merge ethnic studies and pedagogy are asking, "Why weren't we taught this history?" and "Why should I be made to feel ashamed of who I am and how I speak?" A time when there is no denying that the decisions we make as teachers reflect our stance on whether we seek to engage students in an education that will bring about conformity or freedom (Freire, 1970). My hope is that the writers in our class feel supported in an environment that sees them as active participants in their learning, through transformative writing experiences, helping them not only connect with the world but also have a say in shaping it. We need those critical youth voices more than ever. The time is now.

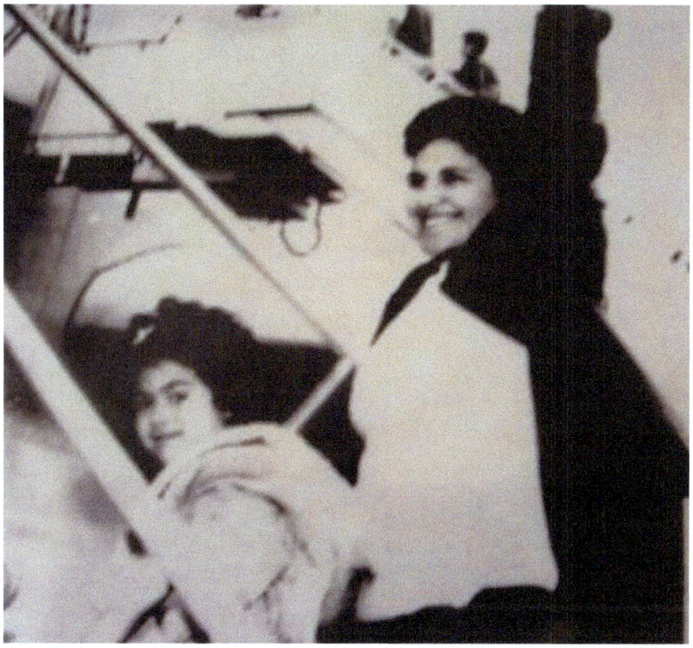

Chapter Two

Soy de aquí y de allá: Migration, Immigration, and Moves That Upend Lives

I came here on March 24, 2013, so I literally spent the last two months or three of fourth grade here. The transition was pretty hard because everything is different. You never expect to have that change, especially in how people are going to treat you.

—Jenifer, undergraduate student in Childhood Education with a Bilingual Extension

Jenifer was one of five college students taking courses in ethnic studies and teacher preparation that I interviewed for a bicoastal (New York and California) study on the impact of Latinx children's literature on bilingual teacher preparation (España, Herrera & Sánchez Hernández, forthcoming). Jenifer was one of three students from the Dominican Republic, and the other two students based in New York had parents from Guatemala and Ecuador. Interviews, focus groups, and class artifacts revealed the impact of immigration transitions on their lives and how they keep this close to their hearts as they develop instruction for their school sites (all were working in schools either as teacher assistants, through fieldwork observations, or student teaching). Although the study focused on children's literature, the (im)migration theme was everywhere. It was a lens that these future teachers were carrying in their interactions with students in New York City and with their own families. When we read the picture book *Beauty Woke* by NoNieqa Ramos, illustrated by Paola Escobar, they talked about the power in that Puerto Rican family connection and intervention when the protagonist internalizes society's negative messages about her and people like her. In being inclusive of communities living under colonization, like Puerto Rico's status with the United States, we use the parenthesis around "im" for (im)migration, noting the movement of people across these contested political boundaries.

For over thirty years, Mexican American journalist, author, and executive producer of the *Latino USA* podcast, Maria Hinojosa has been telling the stories of migrants. On the *Latino USA* podcast episode "Still Hopeful: Immigration Over 30 Years," Maria Hinojosa says the following:

> I think about all of the stories that I've heard time and time again, covering this story for thirty years here on *Latino USA*. And yes, some things have changed. But many things, too many things, have not: like the constant anti-immigrant rhetoric, no comprehensive immigration reform since 1986, and the fact that the journeys that people take here have gotten increasingly dangerous. I don't know, I just thought that after thirty years of this, that people would realize that immigrants are not a threat to this country. That immigrants are not the ones who are bringing violence into this country. I would've thought that, by now, people would see that immigrants, refugees, migrants are actually the superhumans, the ones that can survive things that we could never even imagine in New York: climbing through the jungle, riding the Beast, dealing with the violence on the part of immigration officials in Mexico and the United States. To me, the story should be that these are the people who believe the possibilities of anything that could happen. And that, that fills me with extraordinary hope. I just wish the rest of the city and country could see that.
>
> (Hinojosa, 2023)

My father benefitted from the immigration reform in 1986, which Maria Hinojosa mentions. I reside in New York State, a state I have called home since I turned five years old, when my mother brought me to the United States from Chile to be reunited with my dad in 1987. Like the students in that bicoastal research study, my immigrant experience shapes how I approach my teaching. Like Maria Hinojosa, who interviewed migrants outside of The Roosevelt Hotel (turned into an arrival center for asylum seekers in early 2023) in New York City, learning of their journeys (Hinojosa, 2023), I often wonder about my students and their families' transitions here, asking myself:

- "Do my students feel welcomed?"
- "Are there assumptions about their countries of origin and the decision to migrate I need to unpack?"
- "Are there texts that reflect their journeys and open their minds to others'?"
- "How were their families' experiences with schools in the past, and how can I learn more about them to nurture a positive relationship with our classroom and school?"

I also wrestle with the tension students and their families experience, especially those seeking asylum in a city and country that has more dehumanizing messages from political leaders and the general public who are either unaware or do not care about the U.S. intervention in their home countries that has pushed hundreds of thousands of migrants across decades seeking refuge. With children migrating and starting a new life and school, their lives are disrupted, and that instability often continues when they begin school. For example, I write at a time when migrant families in New York City are required to apply for a new shelter after sixty days (Jorgensen, 2024). Children face changes in school life and home life, and it is our responsibility as educators to prepare welcoming spaces for them in our classrooms and to provide ample migration and immigration narratives to open up the limited worldviews of those who have no idea what migrants go through or why they are coming here in the first place.

Haitian author Edwidge Danticat wrote *Behind the Mountains*, a middle-grade novel about immigration from Haiti, over two decades ago and in a recent reprint of the book says the following:

> Since this book was published, U.S. immigration has increasingly been mired in scapegoating and stigmatization. Children have risked life and limb to cross borders alone to come to this country, and when traveling with their parents, they have—in some cases—been separated from them. There are so many stories of immigrant children

> and families that remain untold, stories that desperately need to be told. My hope is also that this book will inspire others to tell their own stories. I believe that with each story we share, we become stronger, and with each story we read (or receive), we become just a little bit wiser. To quote a proverb that Celiane did not mention, but is one of my favorites, Piti piti zwazo fè nich. Little by little, the bird builds its nest. Let's build a nest of stories together.
>
> (Danticat, 2022)

I continue to write about my immigration story and encourage my students (and you) to explore these journeys. I wrote the poem "Remember Me" at the Fall 2022 Latinx In-Community Retreat for Writers at the Highlights Foundation. Young adult author Alex Villasante shared prompts with us each morning. One morning, our prompt was: *What would you tell your younger self if you wanted them to know something you know now?*

This writing prompt is helpful to consider one particular moment in time and what you'd like younger you to know. In this case, I thought about my immigration journey and what it has looked like, from the moment I came to the United States from Chile to the transitions with language, family, friends, and community. There were many things I did not understand when my parents decided to start a new life in the United States, leaving everything familiar behind in Chile. There is an entire history of Chile's relationship with the United States, specifically the CIA's involvement in the military coup of September 11, 1973, that impacted my family and, to this day, is a part of our story that is not addressed at family gatherings. As I did in this poem, consider how your body has carried something from childhood.

Leaving Chile with my mom in 1987

As you read through my personal writing that opens this chapter and all the chapters across this book, think about how inviting students to share experiences through writing (their own or ones they are learning about in their studies) can offer transformative connections to help nurture their identities as writers—or writer identity—in their lives and in writing lessons like the ones that follow.

Poem: "Remember Me"

Remember me
before the clenching of your jaw,
the grinding of teeth,
living without papers, with uncertainty.
Will we ever see our family?

Remember me
clutching the Care Bears lunch box across airports,
a decision not your own,
to leave la tierra que te vio nacer, all that you know,
joining papá en Nueva York.

Remember me
before English gnawed away at your insides,
the way to make your teacher smile,
to make your parents proud.
Who knew the silencing of Spanish could be so loud?

Remember me
before religion's chokehold on memory,
limiting who and how we could love,
the "eso no es de Dios,"
euphemisms for "there is no room for that in the Lord's home."

Remember me
as you walk in gratitude for the family you've created:
tíos de Argentina—your first neighbors in Queens—
amigas de El Salvador y Guatemala—singing with you in the church's worship team.
Caribbean students, teachers, and friends embodying a supportive community.

Remember me
and breathe.
You no longer have to try to hold it all in.
Immigrant children trying to meet the expectations of many:
You are not your resiliency.

Personal Narrative: "The Layover"

In "The Layover," I write about that moment that changed my life forever: the time we left Chile for the United States. It's a moment I return to often in my thoughts and writing. I've workshopped it with countless middle-grade students and teachers during my narrative writing teaching demonstrations. When creating narrative writing lessons, my colleagues and literacy coach would consider the different writing strategies to help students come up with their favorite moments. Some included lists of essential places, people, and life issues. It helped me to return to my writing notebook and notice the common threads across my lists. Chile, my mom, and immigration were most prevalent in my writing. I've known for a long time that this is one of the life-defining moments and that writing about it would help me understand it better. It is also the moment most talked about in family gatherings. In these last few years, when I've lived with my parents in a multi-generational home, it is also the story I ask most questions about. It continues to open up new possibilities for understanding our immigration journey.

I carried the Care Bears lunch box that tía Flor gave me at our goodbye party the night before, while mamá clutched the bag with my medicine in one hand and grabbed my little hand with her other sweaty palm. In the last ten hours, we had been in two airports: Santiago, Chile, and New York City. Mamá attempted a smile as I gasped when I saw the planes through the windows. "¿Dónde está papá?" I asked repeatedly. "¡Ya calladita, mi hijita!" mamá responded with a stern whisper, trying to get me to be quiet. She took deep breaths, looked at the planes, and then back at me. "¿Cuándo lo vamos a ver?" again, I could not let it go. I was almost five years old and remembered the great party from the night before, where the family sent us off on our adventure to reunite with papá. I didn't understand why mamá wasn't expressing that same enthusiasm. I was practically skipping through the airport terminal. Mamá walked at a slow and uncertain pace. I looked at every person around us to see if it was my papito lindo. Mamá looked at signs and doors.

The family decided not to tell me the whole story. For days, I was told we would see my papá. Neighbors, family, and friends in my tío's panaderías wished us well on our trip. There was so much laughter and singing in our fiesta de despedida that I could practically see papá there with us when the reality was that it had been over a year. But this reunion with papá in New York City wasn't as simple as my five-year-old brain had imagined. I thought we would get off the plane and papá would be there. I also had no awareness of immigration policy, separated families, and why some families would make drastic decisions to be together, some undergoing an undocumented path.

I let go of my mamá's hand and ran down a long corridor. I was tired of strangers, tired of planes, tired of waiting. A man in uniform started making his way towards us. Mamá quickly grabbed me, and I could feel her shaking. As the man in the uniform approached, mamá reminded me, "pórtate bien y tranquilita." He walked over, said a few words in English, patted my head, and left. It was too brief of an interaction for us to process, and I was just confused because I had no idea what he said. Mamá stood there, breathing heavily and leaning against the wall. What could've made her so afraid?

"¿Mamá, qué pasa?," I asked, trying to get an explanation. But she didn't say a word. Instead, we walked. Her pace quickened. She no longer looked at signs. She no longer lingered to let me wonder and ask for papá. She walked faster until we suddenly went through massive revolving doors and stared at a line of yellow cars. A chilly fall breeze hit our faces. As we took a few steps toward the yellow cars, I looked behind me to catch the sun and a row of flags waving as if to say, "hola, bienvenida," welcoming me to this country. I squinted as I tried to find the Chilean flag. But there was no time. Mamá and I got into one of the yellow cars. She gave the driver a card with an address, took a deep breath, turned to me, and said, "vamos a ver a tu papá," "let's go see your dad."

Avenida Perú in Viña del Mar, Chile, July 10, 1986

TEACHER TEXT SET

Media

- Documentaries: *Harvest of Empire, We Still Here, Immigration Nation*
- Podcasts: *La Brega, Latino USA, Radio Ambulante*
- Videos: "Afro-Indigenous Poet Alan Pelaez Lopez Breaks Down Why Blackness is Radical in Latinidad" and "Breaking Down the Anti-Blackness of Latinidad" with Felice León on *The Root*

Articles

- "The Coloniality of Disaster: Race, Empire, and the Temporal Logics of Emergency in Puerto Rico, USA" by Yarimar Bonilla
- "Let Puerto Rico be Free" by Jaquira Díaz
- "Talking to My Family about Colorism is an Act of Self-Love" by Lilliam Rivera

Informational Books

- *Harvest of Empire* by Juan Gonzalez
- *An African American and Latinx History of the United States* by Paul Ortiz
- *Aftershocks of Disaster: Puerto Rico Before and After the Storm* by Yarimar Bonilla and Marisol LeBrón
- *Racial Innocence: Unmasking Latino Anti-Black Bias and the Struggle for Equality* by Tanya Katerí Hernández
- *The Dark Fantastic: Race and the Imagination from Harry Potter to the Hunger Games* by Ebony Elizabeth Thomas
- *Octavia's Brood: Science Fiction Stories from Social Justice Movements* edited by adrienne maree brown and Walidah Imarisha

Social Media Accounts

Al Otro Lado: @alotrolado_org
CUNY—Initiative on Immigration and Education: @cuny_iie
The Immigration Coalition: @theimmigrationcoalition
Immigration Equality: @immigrationequality
Migration Policy Institute: @migrationpolicyinstitute
Investigative journalist, Bianca Graulau: @Biancagraulau
AfroLatino Forum: @afrolatinoforum
Ain't I Latina: @aintilatina
Dash Harris: @DiasporaDash
Felice León: @felicexleon
Latinx Racial Equity Project: @latinxracialequityproject

LESSON SEQUENCE OVERVIEW AND STUDENT TEXT SET "Soy de aquí y de allá": Migration, Immigration, and Moves That Upend Lives			
Lesson #1	**Lesson #2**	**Lesson #3**	**Lesson #4**
We Still Here documentary trailer Investigative journalist Bianca Graulau's documentary *Aquí Vive Gente* on Bad Bunny's "El Apagón" music video (begins at 4:35 minutes) *Sí, Se Puede: The Latino Heroes Who Changed the United States* graphic novel by Julio Anta, illustrated by Yasmín Flores Montañez	Ariana Brown's "23" spoken word poetry performance Conversation: "Afro-Mexican Poetics" conversation and poetry readings with Alan Pelaez Lopez and Ariana Brown Darrel Alejandro Holnes' "Amending Wall" poem on the *Poetry Unbound* podcast	"Crane Poem Gallery" and "Sanctuary Breakfast" by Aida Salazar in *Land of the Cranes* *Imagine* by Juan Felipe Herrera (poem, picture book or video) *Hear My Voice/ Escucha mi voz: The Testimonies of Children Detained at the Southern Border of the United States* (book trailer)	*The Grief Keeper* by Alexandra Villasante Latinx KidLit Book Festival "Fantastical y Más Fuerte: Contemporary Takes on Immigration" video

Lesson #1: (Im)migration: A Multimodal Introduction

Although my work has been mostly with middle-grade and college students, one of the highlights was my teaching journey with a second-grade team in El Barrio, New York. We met every Thursday to plan and taught together for a year and a half. I was definitely out of my comfort zone! Second graders wanted hugs and were mesmerized by every word we shared in our read-alouds and writing lessons. In the fall of 2017, one of those students joined the class from Puerto Rico. His Puerto Rican teacher welcomed him, and we did our best to help him with the transition. This second grader had lost his grandfather to Hurricane Maria, which had hit Puerto Rico only a few weeks before he arrived at The Bilingual Bicultural School in Spanish Harlem. His teacher had family on the island, and it was a really difficult time for everyone who expected the United States government to do more to help with recovery efforts. We focused our energy on welcoming the newly arrived children from Puerto Rico and teaching the rest of the class about their island home.

Thanks to the creative ways activists and journalists are using social media, we now have more access to information about Puerto Rico, and other colonized places that continue to face injustice and displacement. Places where people have deep connections to the lands of their ancestors and are forced to make difficult decisions when they are pushed out. Places where families are separated and where migration is an unfortunate inevitability for some. This lesson sequence begins with a multimodal immersion into migration from the perspective of Puerto Ricans. We move into a discussion on borders and identity with poets Ariana Brown, Alan Pelaez Lopez, and Darrel Alejandro Holnes. Middle-grade author Aida Salazar and young adult author Alex Villasante help us consider the topic of immigration through fiction, inspiring our own stories and poems that consider the impact of (im)migration and the ways we speak back.

WRITING LESSON #1

LESSON TEXTS

- *We Still Here* (Jacobs-Fantauzzi, 2022) documentary trailer
- Investigative journalist Bianca Graulau's documentary *Aquí Vive Gente* at the end of Bad Bunny's "El Apagón" music video [begins at 4:35 minutes]
- *Sí, Se Puede: The Latino Heroes Who Changed the United States* graphic novel by Julio Anta, illustrated by Yasmín Flores Montañez

OBJECTIVES

Discussion: Discuss the reasons why migrants leave their homeland for the United States and how the United States has been involved in destabilizing regions.

Text Analysis: Use transitions such as "Because," "Today," "The result is ..." in analyzing history and the present.

Writing: Use the prompt "In the past, when I thought of/saw/heard _____, I used to immediately associate it with _____. I realized I needed to learn more when I ..."

OPENING DISCUSSION

Show the documentary trailer for *We Still Here* (Jacobs-Fantauzzi, 2022) and discuss the repeated mention of what Hurricane Maria revealed, how it "unveiled the reality that was underneath the surface." What was the government response (or lack thereof) after Hurricane Maria? What was revealed? How did the community of Comerío, Puerto Rico come together?

TEXT ANALYSIS

Show the documentary *Aquí Vive Gente,* featured at the end of Bad Bunny music video for the song "El Apagón" (the documentary begins at 4:35 minutes). Focus on the following excerpt from the documentary [12:45–14:05]:

> Martin G. Brumbaugh School is one of the more than 600 schools the government of Puerto Rico has closed in the past ten years. [Don't close the school! Don't close the school!] Now this school will be an apartment building with a sea view ... Many properties bought by beneficiaries are then dedicated to tourism ... Because the United States invaded and took possession of Puerto Rico by the end of the 19th century, U.S. sugar companies were enabled to take over the land. They hired Puerto Ricans as workers and paid them low wages that kept them in poverty. Today, Puerto Rico is still a U.S. possession, and these incentives give Americans an advantage and invite them to buy properties in Puerto Rico. These properties frequently become vacation rentals under the promise of service industry jobs for the local population. The result is a foreign owner that hoards all the profits.
>
> Bianca Graulau, Puerto Rican investigative journalist

The documentary begins with the experiences of the residents of Comerío, Puerto Rico, who face eviction notices, and investigative journalist Bianca Graulau explains how beneficiaries of Act 22 (a tax incentive) take advantage of that law, something that local residents cannot benefit from. Facilitate analysis of this part of the documentary, noticing how Bianca Graulau connects a current injustice (school closures and real-estate benefits for wealthy non-Puerto Ricans) with the past. Notice the transitions used to help the audience follow the argument:

- "Because the United States invaded and took possession of Puerto Rico ..."
- "Today, Puerto Rico is still a U.S. possession ..."
- "The result is ..."

WRITING

Part One: Students (in groups, partnerships, or as a class) can collaborate to create a list of the protest signs or phrases shown in the film. Some are chants we hear or lines on signs from protesters, others are on community murals. For example:

- "Las playas no se venden" [5:39]
- "U.S. colonial property" [5:44]
- "P.R. no se vende" [5:49]
- "La unión hace la fuerza" [5:50]
- "Fuera policía" [5:51]
- "Acabaron las promesas" [5:51]
- "Aquí vive gente cosechando futuro" [9:28]
- "¡No la cierren! ¡No la cierren! ¡No la cierren!" [12:53]
- "Puerto Rico se defiende" [21:14]
- "Las playas son del pueblo" [21:18]

Part Two: Show students how you identify one protest line and use the prompt "In the past, when I thought of/saw/heard _____ I used to immediately associate it with _____. I realized I needed to learn more when I ..." Reflecting on the documentary with this prompt helps students process their learning and prepare for the writing tasks in the upcoming lessons. For example, see my reflection below:

"¡No la cierren!"

Children protesting in their schoolyard chanting "Don't close the school!" is one of the most impacting images and audio I'll remember from the documentary. In the past, when I thought of Puerto Rico, I used to immediately associate it with the beach. I realized I needed to learn more when I saw the connection between closed schools turned beachfront property and locals displaced. "¡No la cierren!" or "Don't close it!" is a call for justice. Justice for the children who attend those schools, justice for the local community members who have formed part of that community for decades, and justice for the grassroots organizers who are speaking back to the government officials and others who benefit from selling out the Puerto Ricans on the island.

CLOSING DISCUSSION

Inspiration from *Sí, Se Puede: The Latino Heroes Who Changed the United States* graphic novel by Julio Anta, illustrated by Yasmín Flores Montañez.

Julio Anta's graphic novel features Latinx figures, including athletes, artists, activists, astronauts, and more! It is a great transition from watching *Aquí Vive Gente*, especially considering the images of protest. Students can examine a few pages on a figure or a topic to learn more about past and present-day changemakers. This is a great way to provide closure to a discussion on Puerto Rico, protest, and migration. Julio is Puerto Rican and Colombian, and illustrator Yasmín Flores Montañez is also Puerto Rican. This is also a helpful text for informational writing and graphic design, as students consider texts with biographical information and illustrations that teach readers about a person or a time period.

Lesson #2: (Im)migration: Poetry

When I taught in a sixth-grade bilingual dual language Spanish-English class, I was inspired by how motivated my students became during our poem of the week, poet of the month, and poetry units. I knew this was not the norm, as many teacher friends would share how jaded their students were when introduced to anything related to poetry. We found that, for many of them (students and teachers), poetry had been taught as a to-do list, where they checked off the times they used a specific literary device. It wasn't about seeing the world differently or feeling deeply. It was about fulfilling a checklist for assignments.

In *En Comunidad: Lessons for Centering the Voices and Experiences of Bilingual Latinx Students* (2020), coauthor Luz Yadira Herrera and I develop another way of integrating poetry throughout the school year and consider how poetry can be engaged with as a class to consider what it teaches us, how it is a way of resistance (to dominant narratives, false narratives), and how it can be one path toward healing (more on this in Lesson #3 with a middle-grade novel in verse). What would it feel like for students to be immersed in poetry throughout the school year, so they have a plethora of mentors when the time comes for them to write their own? What would it feel like for adults to feel encouraged by the many poets surrounding us, especially those helping us make sense (or ask questions alongside us) of our reality?

WRITING LESSON #2

LESSON TEXTS

- Ariana Brown's "23" spoken word poetry performance
- Conversation: "Afro-Mexican Poetics" conversation and poetry readings with Alan Pelaez Lopez and Ariana Brown
- Darrel Alejandro Holnes' "Amending Wall" poem on the *Poetry Unbound* podcast

OBJECTIVES

Discussion: Discuss the perspectives on Blackness and Latinidad.

Text Analysis: Track how the speaker is impacted by the ways others perceive them and how they respond.

Writing: Use the prompt "I was _____ years old when I first _____" to write a poem.

OPENING DISCUSSION

1. Part One: Read the short bios of the two poets featured in our lesson: Alan Pelaez Lopez and Ariana Brown. Share one observation from your reading of the biographies and ask students to share their observations. For example, you might notice the role of place in the poets' lives (where they are from, where they currently reside), while students might observe the poets' focus, where they studied, and what they do now for a living. Some might also notice the language they use (notice Alan's inclusive language in Spanish, too, in their bio).
2. Part Two: Watch an excerpt from "Afro-Mexican Poetics" (Pelaez Lopez, 2020), a conversation between Alan Pelaez Lopez and Ariana Brown when they respond to the following question: "When did you realize you were Afro-Mexicano? or Black?" [at 1:03:05–1:08:25]. Discuss reactions to the responses to that question. Students can share their realizations. For example, they can work from identity webs or lists of groups they identify with (race, ethnicity, gender, sexuality, nationality, geographical region, hobby/interests) and follow up with when they first realized they were part of that group.

TEXT ANALYSIS

Play Ariana Brown's poem "23" and share observations.

Revisit the following line on language: "Grandma, I'm learning anyways that language is a belonging." Ask students to use the "language is a belonging" line as inspiration to share how they'd finish the sentence "Language is _____." You can facilitate this conversation by noticing how students complete the sentences. Are their descriptions positive or negative? Do they view language as a process or something static? Ask students to elaborate their lines in small groups or partnerships to give you time to synthesize their lines, noticing patterns or differences.

Ariana ends the poem with lines about her name and how she was given a name that could be said in Spanish and in English. What are our students' name stories? For some, their names are a source of pride and connection. It may be the opposite for others, as they feel disconnected and not fully themselves. Allow students to discuss their name story or someone else's (it can be someone in their family, a friend, or a celebrity)*. Ariana Brown's name story is connected to language, and they may also have this connection. Ask students to share in groups to see commonalities and differences in their name stories. Does language play a role in their name stories? Why or why not? Have their connections to their names shifted? Why or why not?

*As always, we defer to students' comfort with themselves and the classroom community when sharing. Therefore, some may not yet feel comfortable sharing their own name story and may defer to sharing what they know of someone else or ask their classmates to share.

WRITING

Borrowing a Line: "I Was _______ Years Old When I First _______"

Part One: Begin by sharing a list of the first times you were made aware of something about your identity or a group you belonged to during your childhood/teen years. For example, my list includes:

- I was five years old when I first learned what it meant to be undocumented (undocumented immigrant identity).
- I was five years old when I first came to have friends from different parts of the world (a newcomer student from Chile in New York City).
- I was ten years old when I first learned what living as a documented resident meant (documented immigrant identity).
- I was fifteen when I realized my church leader would not support me attending a non-Christian college (Evangelical Christian).

Part Two: Ask students to return to that list from the opening discussion and elaborate to include different groups/identities.

Part Three: Show students how you take one idea from the prompt and turn it into a poem by first writing sensory details of that moment (what you heard, what you saw) in a small-moment narrative and later turning it into a poem by creating rhythm using line breaks.

For example, the first draft of my writing (in the form of a small-moment narrative or anecdote) might look like the following:

"I was five years old when I first learned what it meant to be undocumented. I had been in the United States for just a few days when I went shopping with my mom. It was a cold fall day, and every step we took in this new neighborhood, new country, and new land seemed like an eternity. We never made it to the big shopping mall in our neighborhood because we got lost. I thought my mom would do what adults always do, ask for help. Instead, my mom held my hand and fought back the tears. We walked on Queens Boulevard, and I wondered why we couldn't just ask the people on the street for directions to the mall or how to get back home. I can't quite remember if my mom explained why we couldn't ask for help (because we couldn't get caught). We didn't have the papers to be in this country, and we had to be careful, or else we could be sent back to Chile and be separated from my dad."

My second draft might look like this if I consider how to emphasize sensory details and create rhythm with line breaks:

At five, I (somewhat) first learned the meaning of
undocumented.
A shopping trip turned terrifying.
Fears of family separation looming on the Queens Boulevard horizon.
My puzzled looks.
Why can't we ask for help?
My mamá's "está bien mi'jita."
Calming words mixed with a tightened grip.
A mother's sweaty palm and a child's confused gaze.
We eventually made our way.
Back to this new home.
Back to the comfort of a basement apartment.
Back to neighbors who spoke Spanish and helped us feel
welcomed.
Would all outings be like this?
At five, I (somewhat) first learned the meaning of
fear—
family separation after reunification—
and the courageous love of a family that would do anything to be
together.

If it's not already a part of your writing community, encourage students to collect their writing (digital notebook, folder, notepad, journal) so they can return to it periodically. For instance, we'll return to this poem when we study the topic of mental health in the Latinx community in Chapter 3.

CLOSING DISCUSSION: Response Poem and Analysis

Students can listen to the *Poetry Unbound* podcast episode on Panamanian poet Darrel Alejandro Holnes' poem "Amending Wall." *Poetry Unbound* host, Pádraig Ó Tuama, reads the poem and explains his connection to the poem and analysis of the craft, from the way this poem is a response to Robert Frost's "Mending Wall" to how it speaks back to the injustice of borders. Pádraig Ó Tuama writes:

> ... for whom is the America that Frost was writing existent, and for whom is the America that he is reflecting in the way that he's spelled it, existing here? It's provocative to do this, and I think it is the job of justice. And he doesn't resolve it. He leaves the question, like a challenge, like an open wound, and invites those of us made comfortable, perhaps, by the imagination of the Frost poem, to become uncomfortable and to feel prompted and moved by the art that he's putting forward.

Students can read the transcript to see how "Amending Wall" responds to "Mending Wall," noticing similarities and differences. They can discuss how "Amending Wall" is a commentary on borders and US immigration policy. They can also play around with words to notice how their poem "I Was ______ Years Old When I First ______" is a response to Ariana Brown's poem "23."

Lesson #3: (Im)migration: Middle-Grade Literature

"Translanguaging refers to the language practices of bilingual people," writes Ofelia García in the City University of New York–New York State Initiative on Emergent Bilinguals (CUNY-NYSIEB) translanguaging guide for educators (2012). How can we describe how we use different varieties of languages as bilingual and multilingual people? The term "translanguaging" came into my life during my teacher preparation studies as I learned to describe how my bilingual students communicated. I later learned about the translanguaging pedagogy I implemented, which included strategies to help students grow in their bilingualism and understand the content in the classroom. It helped me to see that those rigid language boundaries (seen in different places in society, even in some bilingual programs) made no sense to me. I taught students from across the Caribbean, Mexico, and Central America, and even those from the same country spoke different varieties of Spanish. Add my Chilean Spanish to the mix, and we had a vibrant linguistic diversity in my sixth-grade classroom! Not only were we learning ways to call things in our different varieties of Spanish (and English) but also to accept our bilingualism, to move away from the shame that comes in an English-dominant society, and towards a multilingual lens on life.

The texts we engage our students with set the tone for how we view language or how our language ideologies shape our teaching, especially when discussing topics like migration and immigration with Latinx students.

WRITING LESSON #3

LESSON TEXTS

- "Crane Poem Gallery" and "Sanctuary Breakfast" by Aida Salazar in *Land of the Cranes* (2020)
- *Imagine* by Juan Felipe Herrera (poem, picture book or video)
- *Hear My Voice/ Escucha mi voz: The Testimonies of Children Detained at the Southern Border of the United States* (book trailer)

OBJECTIVES

Discussion: Identify the ways the topics of migration and immigration come up in different texts and experiences in our lives.

Text Analysis: Compare perspectives in the text.

Writing: Build off of writing partner/group discussions to write poems about an object that reveals a connection with someone meaningful to the writer.

OPENING DISCUSSION

Show the *Land of the Cranes* book trailer on the Scholastic YouTube channel (2020). Discuss what the class already knows about the book or the topics of migration, immigration, and family separation, using the following guiding questions as needed:

1. What do we know about migration?
2. How have the texts you've read up to this point in your lives at schools talked about migration?
3. What is the difference between migration and immigration?
4. What image comes to mind when you think of migration or immigration? Why?

TEXT ANALYSIS

Read the poem "Crane Poem Gallery."

First Read (teacher-directed reading and conversation):

When preparing to read the poem, note how the words move across the page, how the structure connects to the title, and the themes in the book trailer.

In "Crane Poem Gallery," Betita describes Papi's way of speaking as "Spanish-sounding English warm soft round words." She notes that the principal tried to correct Betita's own "singsong East LA English," while her teacher Ms. Martinez "never cared one speck about" the way she spoke (p. 2). Consider the different sounds, words, idioms, and expressions that you've heard in one or more languages. How do people react to different kinds of English and Spanish? Why might someone react like the principal instead of the teacher's more welcoming approach?

Second Read (student-directed reading):
Ask students to take on different stanzas as they join in during a second read of the poem.

Third Read (student-directed reading):
Have students read and discuss the poem as they notice the "Spanish-sounding English" description of Papi's question, the "singsong East LA English" description of the way Betita speaks, and how the poem describes Betita's poet identity.

Read the poem "Sanctuary Breakfast":
With this second poem, you may want to focus on how the author creates tension by noticing the dialogue, revealing actions, and inner thinking around the topic of immigration. What is happening in their community (raids)? How does the family talk (or not talk) about it? What questions does Betita ask? How do the parents respond to the child's questions?

WRITING

Writing partner/group discussion

To best transition from discussion to writing, groups can fill out the following Poetry as Teaching, Resistance, and Healing (España & Herrera, 2020) graphic (Appendix B) with their observations on what the poems teach us (about immigration, language, and family), how the poems resist harmful dominant narratives, and the ways these poems can help in our healing journeys.

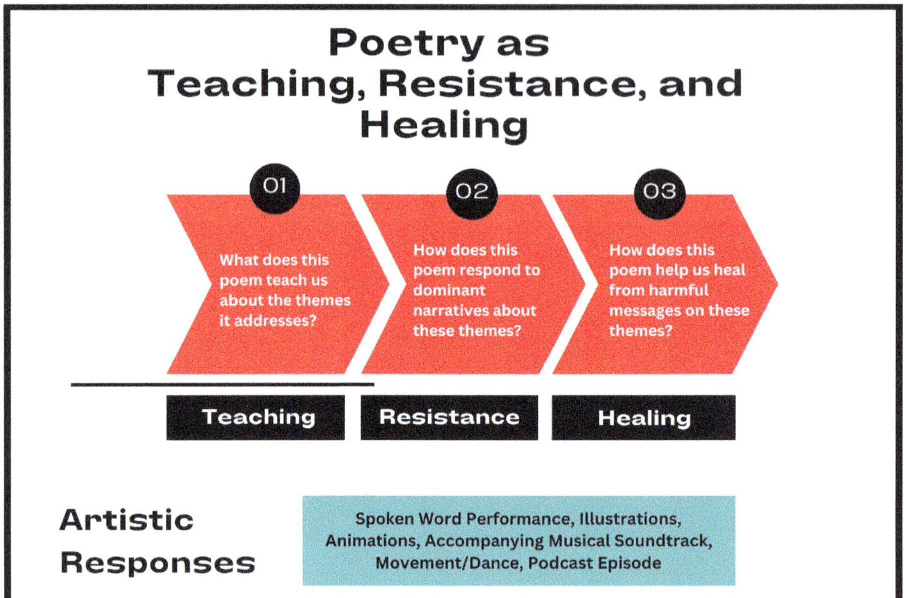

Adapted from ***En Comunidad: Lessons for Centering the Voices and Experiences of Bilingual Latinx Students*** **by Carla España and Luz Yadira Herrera (2020)**

Write

Students can consider the artistic responses in the Poetry as Teaching, Resistance, and Healing graphic if necessary to work on a poem (individually or with a partner) that reveals that connection with their special someone through an object. For example, in my poem "Mujeres en mi altar" or "Women On My Altar," I think of multiple objects making up one special space—the altar—where I honor three extraordinary women in my life. Teachers can share their poems, and students can work on translations with a partner.

"Mujeres en mi altar"	"Women On My Altar"
Mujeres	Women
que me protegen,	who protect me,
me guían,	guide me,
me motivan,	motivate me,

me levantan,
me recuerdan de la fuerza
que tengo porque caminan conmigo.

Mujeres
con sus mantas,
joyas, y plantas.
Conectadas al mar,
la tierra,
el aire,
sus cuerpos, y familia.

Abuelita Flor,
con sus manos
sacaba los dolores de nues-
tros cuerpos,
remedios caseros salían de su cocina.
Un cucurucho, periódico puesto
a nuestros oídos.
Un té para los dolores menstruales.

Tía Marcela,
con su don de contar cuentos
animaba a medio mundo.
Cuando se iba con un pololo,
rompiendo reglas
de comportamiento de una
"señorita."

Nonna Aida,
caminábamos tomadas de las manos
por Jackson Heights, Queens
después de mi día escolar,
crujiendo palabras en inglés,

lift me up,
remind me of the strength
I carry because they walk with me.

Women
with their shawls,
jewels, and plants.
Connected to the sea,
land,
air,
their bodies, and family.

Abuelita Flor
cleared our physical pains
with her hands,
home remedies from her kitchen.
A cone of newspaper over
our ears.
A tea for menstrual cramps.

Tía Marcela,
motivating us all
with her gift of storytelling.
When she'd leave with
her boyfriend,
breaking rules of how a
"young woman" should
be.

Nonna Aida,
we'd walk hand in hand
through Jackson Heights, Queens
after school,
crunching words in English,

buscando ingredientes para
    un charquicán
chileno.

Las siento cuando
cuido mis plantas,
aprendo de hierbas
y sus poderes para aliviar el dolor,
al cantar, cocinar y escribir.

Adelante seguimos juntas.
¿Cómo fortalecer esta práctica,
esta conexión renovada
que la religiosidad
    sofocante de mi juventud
impidió?

Prenderé las velas.
Llenaré de agua sus envases en el altar.
Cuidaré de mis plantas,
aprenderé de hierbas,
cantaré, cocinaré y
    escribiré nuestras historias.

seeking ingredients to
    make charquicán,
the way she made it Chile.

I sense their presence when
I care for my plants,
learn about herbs
and their healing powers,
as I sing, cook, and write.

We move forward together.
How do I strengthen this practice,
this renewed connection
once suffocated by the
    religiosity of my
    childhood?

I will light the candles.
Place water in their vases on my altar.
Care for my plants,
learn about herbal medicine,
sing, cook, and write our
stories.

CLOSING DISCUSSION

Option #1:

1. Show the *Hear My Voice/ Escucha mi voz: The Testimonies of Children Detained at the Southern Border of the United States* book trailer (Workman Publishing, 2021) on the Workman Publishing book site.
2. Share with students that this book was compiled of the stories and sworn testimonies of sixty-one children. The children represent Guatemala, Honduras, El Salvador, Venezuela, Ecuador, and Mexico.

3. Discuss what students would like to do with their writing (from this lesson, unit, or discussions on translanguaging or the topic of immigration).
4. Make a list of class ideas (personal journal, an anthology for the classroom or school library, poems displayed in the school, spoken word poetry event, etc.).

Option #2:

1. Read the poem "Imagine" by Juan Felipe Herrera, a poet mentioned in the poem from *Land of the Cranes* (Salazar, 2020). You can show the video of the poet reading it or read it from the picture book *Imagine* (Herrera, 2021) (available in Spanish and English by Candlewick Press).
2. Discuss how the poem made students feel.
3. Make a list of the feelings they experienced throughout the poem, along with the words (and illustrations if looking at the picture book) that evoked those feelings (T-chart).
4. Have students use the poem and images in the picture book (if available) to create their own dream trajectories. This can be a classroom dreams or classroom goals gallery where students write their version of "Imagine," and either illustrate or find images to represent their dreams (places they'd like to visit, people they'd like to help, talents they'd like to hone, etc.).

Lesson #4: Young Adult Literature: Speculative Writing and Immigration

No matter how you take in your news, it is probable that something made the headlines regarding immigration on the day or week that you are reading this chapter. Sometimes, we learn of policies, people apprehended at a border, migrants sharing their stories, advocacy organizations providing support for migrants' transitions, local government making a public statement on immigrants in the community, and newcomer children arriving in schools across the school year as their families seek asylum. Reading speculative fiction that tackles the topic of immigration helps us dream beyond the current reality and process issues of injustice in the present.

One of my sixth graders introduced me to the importance of this genre as a vehicle for commenting on injustices. I often gravitated towards memoirs and realistic fiction, but a student walked up to me with a notebook in a "free writing" / "passion project" I had implemented. It was full of writing. This student wrote a whole book! Although he had arrived from Mexico as a toddler, he remembered (and wrote about) how his and his family's immigration journey impacted their daily lives. His book had elements of the fantastic, reality, and adventure. It was not something I had a unit on (yet) or something I had taught, but this student made sure I knew about this interest and his story. I recently included short stories from *Octavia's Brood: Science Fiction Stories from Social Justice Movements* (2015) as mentor texts for my eighth-grade writers. I am convinced of the importance of creating spaces for youth to dream, to create a better world, and while dreaming, to feel less alone in understanding the dilemmas of our time.

WRITING LESSON #4

LESSON TEXTS

- *The Grief Keeper* (2019) by Alexandra Villasante
- Latinx KidLit Book Festival "Fantastical y Más Fuerte: Contemporary Takes on Immigration" (2020) video

OBJECTIVES

Discussion: Discuss how speculative fiction helps us comment on present-day social issues while dreaming of a different world.

Text Analysis: Examine how we learn about a character's motivations by looking at the function of dialogue, revealing actions, and inner thinking in a narrative text.

Writing: Develop a scene that shows what we know about the impact of immigration policies and the characteristics of speculative fiction.

OPENING DISCUSSION

Option #1: Discuss with students the different reasons why people move across nations/borders and how schools can better support students arriving from another place.

Option #2: Select one or more of the following clips from the Latinx KidLit Book Festival "Fantastical y Más Fuerte: Contemporary Takes on Immigration" (2020) session, focusing on Alex Villasante's responses to the questions on her book *The Grief Keeper* (2019).

- Author Alex Villasante talks about *The Grief Keeper* [minutes 4:50–5:45]
- Villasante's response to question #1: What does home mean for your protagonist? [minutes 11:42–12:53]
- Villasante's response to question #2: Why did you choose to incorporate speculative elements in your story? [minutes 19:10–22:08]
- Villasante's response to question #3: How much of your own experiences influenced the story? [minutes 35:30–37:10]
- Villasante's response to question #5: Where do you get your inspiration for the books you write? [minutes 45:30–47:15]

TEXT ANALYSIS

Read the following excerpts from Chapters 1–4 in *The Grief Keeper* by Alexandra Villasante. Discuss how these excerpts help us understand the protagonist's motivations within the context of what we already know about immigration policy affecting children.

#1

Lunch is almost over. We eat fast so we can have a few minutes together before Gabi goes to her classes and I go to mine. She's in an advanced class because she knows so much English. I sit alone with a guard in a small room meant for babies because there is no one else here in my grade. The guard gives me worksheets to do and books to read. I never take the ones in Spanish. I want to show her, and the people I know are watching on the video cameras mounted on the thin walls, how good an American I can be.

#2

"My name is Mary Schoenbeck. You can call me Mary. I will be conducting your interview. Do you need an interpreter?"

If I needed an interpreter, how would I understand her enough to ask for one? There was a time when I thought I could be an interpreter, working for the government or the UN. Now I only want us to be allowed to stay.

"No, ma'am. I speak English fluently."

This surprises the woman enough that she looks up from her stack of folders. "Good. That makes my job easier ...

"All right. Tell me, in your own words, why are you seeking asylum in the United States?"

#3

"Marisol, what we need you to do is help us test a technology. Kind of like a medicine, one that would help our soldiers get better when their brains have had too much stress." ...

Dr. Deng continues. "We call it the corticotropin transfer system, or CTS. It allows the chemicals, the stress factors—released into the body of a person suffering trauma—to be transferred to another person, a 'clean' subject without the same trauma burden. The memories of the trauma are intact—this is not some kind of mind eraser—but the feelings, deep depression, suicidal thoughts, and perhaps even homicidal thoughts that can be produced after severe trauma are greatly reduced. For the aggrieved person, in a matter of weeks it feels as if the trauma is in the distant past. Painful but vague. Remembered but distant ...

WRITING

Writing partner/group discussion: students can discuss their observations of one scene:

- How does Scene 1 add to what we already know about language learning, bilingualism/multilingualism, identity, and belonging?
- How does the author create a sense of fear and pressure in Scene 2?
- How does Excerpt #3 from Chapter 4 reveal elements of the speculative fiction genre?

Writing partner/group writing: Develop *The Grief Keeper* scenes by considering the following:

- What does the protagonist want?
- What challenges does the protagonist experience?
- How does this speculative fiction setting reflect present-day issues?

For example, in my developing the scene in the second excerpt, I might write:

> "You are so articulate," Mary adds as she scribbles down some notes. I said I spoke English fluently, but I wonder what she expected.
>
> "Yes. My school had English classes," I add. In any other place, a comment like that would get a side-eye from me, but too much is riding on this "credible fear interview." That bothers me, too. What fear would not be credible for us seeking asylum? Do they think people gladly leave their families, everything they know, an entire life gone, and make things up to come into this country? I peek through the small rectangular window on the door and see Gabi making friends. We couldn't be any more different. She doesn't have the weight of the world (or caring for her life) on her shoulders. Nor should she. She is just a child. She should enjoy her childhood, be happy, make friends, progress in that advanced English class, and live. I wonder when I'll get to live, too. I wish we could all do more than survive.

CLOSING DISCUSSION

Option #1: Create a writing feedback guide or checklist in small groups or as a whole class. What characteristics of writing (and this genre) do we see in the excerpts? What writing goals could we set for our writing in this genre? For example, in the writing I tried, I focused on the interaction between Mary and Marisol in the "credible fear interview," specifically on Mary's expectations of Marisol and Marisol's wonderings about the challenge she is facing/taking on to care for herself and her sister. I do not include any speculative fiction elements, so that could be my goal.

Option #2: If you did not watch the Latinx KidLit Book Festival "Fantastical y Más Fuerte: Contemporary Takes on Immigration" session for the opening discussion, you can bring that resource in to wrap up the lesson. Discuss what more we learn about this book, topic, and genre, and the author's writing process.

TESTIMONIO: Anel V. Rivera Guerrero

Doctoral Candidate, Rutgers University

Like Jenifer, the undergraduate student who arrived from the Dominican Republic in the fourth grade, featured at the introduction of this chapter, Anel Rivera, bilingual educator and researcher, also came to New York from the Dominican Republic. I first met Anel when I started my graduate studies in education, and Anel and I were in the same New York City Teaching Fellows cohort. In this testimonio, Anel shares her journey with writing and teaching Latinx teens and offers helpful advice for supporting these brilliant writers and their thoughtful teachers.

ANEL ON HER JOURNEY AS AN EDUCATOR:

I began teaching as a New York City Teaching Fellow with you in 2007, and I would say, probably started well before that ... One of my majors in college was international affairs and political science. Moved to New York, got involved in the State Senate. I was told very, very quickly, trying to influence that field and break into that field as my area focus on behalf of the Senator, that it would be very hard to influence policy without knowing what it was to be a teacher. So I became a fellow. I ended up in Inwood as the Spanish component of the side-by-side dual language program that we had there and I stayed in that role until my third year, where we grew the program into seventh grade. I became the literacy teacher, self-contained, still dual language with my first babies and who now have children of their own.

I felt like there wasn't enough in my master's degree ... I wanted more. So I went, thanks to Yvonne [De Gaetano, former Hunter College, CUNY Bilingual Program Director]. She called Ofelia [García, Professor Emerita, Graduate Center, CUNY]. Ofelia called me over, and I applied, and I got in. I started having children so I had to stop. It's now that I'm finishing. In that process I started teaching in a transitional bilingual middle level and also on the third and fourth grade level in New Jersey. Again, literacy specialization.

And now, once I left that it was full time in academia as a doctoral student and teacher within our language education department, that I'm coming back now to K-12, as the dual language instructional coach for White Plains City School district. In that process working a lot with children with intersectional needs—what we now would say are emergent bilinguals labeled as disabled— advocating for them, learning about them, servicing them as well. That continues to this day. And of course bringing in my expertise as a mother to a child with special needs brings in a lot of information for advocacy, and how to support them, what we can do in classrooms. This has been a lifelong journey, I would say deeply rewarding, deeply challenging … Now, as I continue to advocate in this role outside of the classroom, returning to the community that I was born into, but left for so many years. That has been my greatest evolution.

ANEL ON HER FIRST MEMORY SEEING HERSELF AS A WRITER:

The first memory coming to my mind is fourth grade in this very district, not in this building, but in this district. I wrote a lot of poetry. I don't remember why I started writing poetry … It might have had something to do with my parents' divorce, and it was just a way to then start just to be fully expressive of myself. My mother was at that moment going through a lot, extremely controlling. You know I'm the oldest child, so there's only so much you can say and do without getting in trouble. No one needs to hear what's on my paper and my pen. I journaled a lot as well.

ANEL ON HER FAVORITE WRITING ACTIVITY WITH LATINX TEENS:

Thinking about my time, particularly with middle-school students, when I was in Jersey with my transitional bilingual class, my seventh and eighth graders, I would do two types of activities and the prompts varied but it was the same kind of spirit. I would put up a pretty inflammatory but very mainstream statistic or ideology related to Latinx folks, or to bilingual education, mainly Latinx folks. That was around the time that DACA and DAPA was put out … It was just everywhere, things that you could hear in the hallway. Put it on the board: Do you agree with the statement? Why or why not? What does it make you feel? What can we do about it? And the quantity of languaging and the things that the kids would say, and then we would turn an argument to a writing piece. I remember that year our final project, after doing intense investigation on both sides, bilingually because the media was showing it one way in Spanish, you know. Beautiful moments to be bilingual. They wrote letters to elected officials.

ANEL ON LATINX AUTHORS GIVING HER LIFE RIGHT NOW:

Ofelia's work has always brought life. Nelson [Flores] adds fuel to the fire when it's dying. I'm deeply grateful for him as a mentor, as a professor, as someone on my committee. I'm going to name [María] Cioè-Peña. She is a Latinx author right now that is giving me a lot of life for our emergent bilingual students who are not just SIFE students, but coming in with needs, and we don't have a pathway for them here in the schools. Her research is giving me pathways to advocate for them in an actionable way, in a data-driven way ... She just published a piece about individualized language plans which I started to develop for SIFE students along literacy and math ... Her work, when I feel like it's hopeless, makes me feel hopeful.

ANEL'S ADVICE FOR WRITING TEACHERS OF LATINX YOUTH:

There are many voices we can be inspired by at so many levels, from so many cultures, and ways of being and languaging. It doesn't all have to be perfect or correct. It can be messy and that's beautiful. Metamos la mano en la masa to make this beautiful bread. I wish that when I was growing up, I had seen my histories, I had seen my literature, I had seen my ways of speaking and that that would've been more than OK. That would've been accessible so that it could empower my voice and I could add my voice.

WRITING THAT ANEL IS WORKING ON RIGHT NOW:

I'm working on creating my autoethnography with components of the research. I did it as an example for the research participants. But I'm also journaling a lot to heal myself from everything that I'm going through. So, there, I'm writing for me. I'm writing for my future me so I can remember everything I've gone through, and I'm writing for my daughter, and I'm writing for my son and all the generations that follow so that they can see. That's a generational healing.

Chapter Three

Estamos bien: Talking Mental Health and Breaking Stigmas

"I have a memory that almost discouraged me from speaking Spanish or in a way not make me feel proud of speaking Spanish. When I was in third or fourth grade, a teacher who was the lunch lady and a white woman told me—I had been speaking with an Ecuadorian classmate since there weren't many of us in that school talking about our weekend and catching up—'Oh we're here in the U.S., you're not supposed to talk Spanish, it's only English,' and then just stood there. We were third or fourth graders, so we got scared, and I said, 'maybe we can't speak.'"

—Sara, undergraduate student in Childhood Education with a Bilingual Extension

A multilingual speaker (Quechua, Spanish, and English), undergraduate student, eldest child, family interpreter, and advocate for her younger brother's education, Sara has a lot on her plate. Not only does she navigate life now as a first-generation college student, but she also takes the time to process how best to support the children on her school visits (fieldwork hours required before student teaching). Sara's memory from elementary school reveals the impact of language discrimination on minoritized language speakers. In the bicoastal research-study interview and focus groups (España, Herrera & Sánchez Hernández, forthcoming), Sara proceeded to share how it is only now, as an adult, that she is able to process a lot of those childhood moments that existed alongside a working-class immigrant family's resilience and survival.

In the Vice video "The Kids Are Not Alright: The Mental Health Crisis Affecting Latina Teens" (2020), Latina teens discuss anxiety, depression, suicidal ideation, and the importance of community to support their mental health journeys. Journalist and host Paola Ramos asks, "Is there something about this particular community that makes them more susceptible to anxiety in this very moment?" Dr. Carolina Haussman-Stabile, Assistant Professor of Social Work at Bryn Mawr College, responds:

> We know that first-gen, and especially first-gen in mixed immigration status families—meaning families whose parents might not be documented in the United States and children are—is putting a lot of pressure on this group and is increasing the number of [cases of] anxiety to unseen levels. More than 50 percent of them report anxiety symptoms. I would say that there is a crisis among young Latinas in this context accelerated by political factors, and they themselves, because of normal adolescent development, are facing a lot of stressors in a cultural context that also blames Latinos and stigmatizes being Latina. In a context of a lot of violence. We cannot expect that that will not result in negative outcomes.
>
> (Vice, 2020)

The Center for Disease Control (CDC) Youth Risk Behavior Surveillance System (YRBSS) surveys youth across the United States to learn about their health behaviors, and the latest results are alarming (2021). Forty-three percent of Latina teens surveyed reported that their mental health wasn't good all or most of the time, citing issues such as stress, anxiety, and depression. So, when we see one of the Latina teens in "The Kids Are Not Alright: The Mental Health Crisis Affecting Latina Teens" talk about the importance of her community showing her that she was not alone, we are reminded of the support that these youth need from their local institutions. "First, I thought no one else went through the same thing. I thought it was just me and just being in this group has helped me a lot because hearing other people's emotions and feelings to a problem could also reflect on me because as I went through it, I could be like, they went through it, I could go through it, too." (Vice, 2020). Consider experiences like hers alongside Sara's experience as a first-generation college student, aspiring educator, and family go-to interpreter and advocate for all education matters, and it becomes apparent that these concerns do not exist in isolation. It makes one wonder how organizations like schools, local places of worship, and community centers might use this information to see Latinx teens in a wholistic way and come to understand that they balance not only present-day challenges but also the promise, dreams, and goals they yearn for in their everyday lives.

The title of this chapter, "Estamos bien: Talking Mental Health and Breaking Stigmas," is a play on words from Bad Bunny's song "Estamos Bien," one that he dedicated to the victims of Hurricane Maria when he performed it on the Tonight Show a year after the hurricane devastated the island (2018):

> On September 20, 2017, Puerto Rico was exposed to the full force of nature's ferocity. After one year of the hurricane, there are still people without electricity in their homes. More than 3,000 people died, and Trump's still in denial. ¡Estamos bien y vamos a estar mejor, Puerto Rico!

The song is an affirmation, "we're fine," or "we're doing well," highlighting the resilience of a people in the face of systemic injustice. What's fascinating about this phrase and how Bad Bunny uses it in this context is that "estamos bien" or "estoy bien" is a common way of responding and deflecting when things are not actually going well.

For instance, in the film *Encanto* (Bush et al., 2021), Mirabel Madrigal is the only family member without a gift, but when she sees cracks in the family's enchanted home and tries to warn her Abuela Alma of the dangers to come, she is cast aside. Brushing things off, ignoring reality, or refusing to face some unhealthy practices are ways the family fails to listen to and embrace Mirabel. Instead, when Mirabel tries to warn Abuela, Mirabel sings about not being upset or mad, not feeling regret or sadness, instead forcing herself to say, "I'm fine, I'm totally fine," until she's not and says, "I'm not fine, I'm not fine" (Bush et al., 2021).

That song resonates with so many viewers who feel the tension of pushing certain emotions down but are slowly coming to the realization that we are not fine at all. And how could Mirabel not feel that pressure to ignore things when Abuela Alma tells her (in that same scene at Antonio's celebration), "There is nothing wrong with La Casa Madrigal. The magic is strong" (Bush et al., 2021). Then, just when Mirabel is getting closer to the truth (at least partially as she finds herself at the center of one of her Uncle Bruno's visions), her father, Agustín, sends a similar message about dismissing uncomfortable realities:

> We say nothing. Abuela wants tonight to be perfect 'til the Guzmans leave. You did not break into Bruno's tower, the magic is not dying, the house is not breaking, Luisa's gift is not fading. No one will know. Just act normal. No one has to know.
>
> (Bush et al., 2021)

Where is Mirabel supposed to go? Every person she goes to up to this point in the film has told her to ignore her ominous concerns. Finally, when it is clear that things are not well and the town is worried, Abuela Alma responds, "The magic is strong! EVERYTHING IS FINE! We are the Madrigals!" (Bush et al., 2021). If you come from a family or community that avoids conflict and is hesitant to seek help from mental health professionals to address intergenerational trauma, this movie hits close to home. What pain do we carry? What are the conversations we are avoiding? How are we embarking on paths to healing, especially in the face of what seem like perpetual challenges? Where are the pockets of hope, the people who sustain us, and the policies and institutions ensuring we all have healthcare access?

If we are not well, we cannot teach. If we are not well, we cannot learn. Whether it is caring for family members or facing a transition from another country, school, community, or family setting, or even not feeling at home within our bodies and identities because of the pressures we feel from the outside world, we could all use help to make sure we are mentally healthy. In the poem "Lost on Queens Boulevard," I work through one of my first memories of my mamá expressing a visible sense of fear, something she was great at masking in the days before our move to the United States from Chile.

I was inspired by reading the short story "Eleven" by Sandra Cisneros (1984) with middle-grade students in Harlem, New York. When I became a literacy coach at Don Pedro Albizu Campos School, I found out that "Eleven" was read across several grades. My students shared how connected they felt to the short story, addressing the expectations that adults had of them at that age and of their transitions to New York City from different places in the world, including the Dominican Republic, Mexico, Peru, Puerto Rico, and Yemen. I often think about how our elders in families from underrepresented and underserved communities lacked the support, including mental health support, to process the difficulties in life. The chapter opening picture with my abuelita, Flor, reminds me of this common reality: the family matriarch, mother of ten children, holding it down when my grandfather wasn't around.

Poem: "Lost on Queens Boulevard"

What they don't tell you about coming to la Gran Manzana
is the nostalgia that grows roots from dawn to dusk—
the sweetness of Chile's sunrise greeting you
with manjar on pan amasado from tío Tomás' panadería,
bedtime lullabies preceded by A minor and D minor chords
launching into a cueca classic, "La Consentida."

What you learn about this new life in the Big Apple
is that the love from your parents could tackle any obstacle:
undocumented transition kept as a bittersweet secret from the family,
missing milestones, and masking fears of deportation.

So when you look up and down Queens Boulevard
and don't see the big blue building
papá said would signal you've arrived at the mall—
distracted by your curls swept in the wind from passing cars,
traffic providing that steady, soothing hum like a sleep machine in a baby's
nursery—
know that feeling disoriented is not insurmountable.

Mamá taps into that spidey sense every loving caregiver has,
grips your hand, and takes a series of walks in different directions,
attempting to make it back to your (new) home,
what feels like a safe place where your small family has been reunited.

You patiently await the day when you won't be afraid to ask
"Can you help us? We are lost."
"¿Nos puede ayudar? Estamos perdidas."

Decades later you continue to question
as you're flooded by images and stories of
families in distress,
separated.
Border walls and barbed-wire buoys,
shelter laws and over policing in schools.

What you now know at the core of your soul:
No longer lost.
No longer alone.
Enraged that for some, el sueño americano in la Gran Manzana
rots dreams away.
Yet (for now), you are here to stay.

Personal Narrative: "Para ser bella, hay que ver estrellas"

Remember the trend on social media of people sharing "I was today years old when" as they revealed their new "aha" moments, like how to use a can opener or strainer for pasta? As funny as some of those videos were, I found it a helpful exercise in addressing the things we might otherwise be ignoring. Here's one of my own: I was today years old [meaning forty] when I first learned about the history of beauty standards with hair removal and colonization, thanks to a social media post by Dr. María Cioè-Peña, bilingual educator and faculty member at the University of Pennsylvania. For many of my middle-grade students, feeling "pretty" had meanings tied to what colonizers (and those that internalized these messages) promoted in their countries: straight hair and light skin everywhere they turned. My narrative is titled "Para ser bella, hay que ver estrellas," or "You must see stars in order to be beautiful" (no pain, no beauty/gain). Mamá often said this whenever I was in pain related to some expectation of what it meant to be pretty: the hot blow-dryer to straighten my hair at the Dominican hair salon (how convenient it was to have it three blocks from our church in Washington Heights), the tweezers to remove hair from my eyebrows, or the wax on my legs so I could look "nice" for my fifth-grade graduation.

It was a small room on the second floor of the beauty salon where I thought my problems would be solved. I wasn't getting a haircut or the highlights I always wanted (mamá said I wasn't allowed to change my hair color until I was older). I wasn't even getting a curly cut (in those days, the only cut I got was one with thinning shears). It felt like my own little getaway, far from the noise in Queens. I didn't mind that we were traveling to Chile the next day and had a long list of gifts to get (from the wholesale store with I Love New York items in midtown). All I knew was that I'd get this hair off, and surely, all would be well with the world.

It was my first time saying yes to the question I'd often been asked in the beauty salon, "¿Quieres que te saque el pelo de la cara con cera?" No one ever questioned why anyone would think it was OK to ask a child if they wanted to remove the hair from their face with hot wax. It just seemed like a given. You go in for a cut and blow dry, and leave with hairless chin, sideburns, upper lip, and even forehead. This time, mamá said yes to that question, and I, of course, agreed, happy to get closer to feeling "pretty."

I closed my eyes and felt the hot wax, paper strips, and the cold aloe vera lotion supposed to help the redness and swelling go down after multiple repetitions of the process. "Para ser bella, hay que ver estrellas," my mom reminded me. I cried but remained tight-lipped, sometimes putting my tongue under my upper lip to help them apply the wax and strips. I didn't recognize the person staring back at me in the mirror. Pink-and-red spots scattered across my face where black hair once was. We left that room, and I waited at the salon entrance, embarrassed to go back out in the street with my blotchy face.

About twenty-four hours later, we aren't in New York but in Viña del Mar, Chile. I lay down in a dermatologist's room after the quick thinking of my tía, who made a last-minute appointment for me. The dermatologist walks in and says, "¿Qué caga' te hicieron en la cara?" which roughly translates to "Wtf they do to your face?" My mom proceeded to share an elaborate lie, embarrassed to tell the doctor the truth that I was sitting in his office with a terrible reaction to the hot wax that was placed all over my face the day before to remove my hair. I shook my head and sat up as he examined me with his perplexed look. I left with a prescription for a cream to help with the redness and swelling.

You might be asking why my mom took me to that salon in the first place or didn't take a different approach to my beauty ritual in preparation for a trip back home. Why did the salon staff offer those hair-removal services to a child? Why did the dermatologist not dig deeper into what was happening? Why did I agree to being in pain?" But years before this incident, it was a classmate in third grade who first pointed out to me that the hair on my body was ugly (he was super hairy himself, but that was OK), and I was in fifth grade when my mom's best friend, who was an esthetician in Argentina, first waxed my legs. I was thrilled to wear my fifth-grade graduation dress without hair on my legs as my unwanted accessory. The messaging started early and went across generations; it was rare to hear someone question this, and it was everywhere.

Waiting for the ice cream truck on my block in Queens, New York

TEACHER TEXT SET

1. Media:
   a. GLSEN National School Climate Survey
   b. CDC Youth Risk Behavior Surveillance System Survey
   c. Aspen Institute Community Spotlight: Latinx Youth: Adolescent Mental Health Crisis Dialogue Series
   d. Rocky Mountain PBS interview of Kali Fajardo-Anstine: "Colorado Voices: Latina Author Shares Her Mental Health Journey"
   e. Website: National Alliance on Mental Illness: Compartiendo Esperanza: Mental Wellness in Hispanic/Latin American Community

2. Article:
   a. "More than Nervios" essay by Lilliam Rivera in *Wild Tongues Can't Be Tamed: 15 Voices from the Latinx Diaspora*
3. Books:
   a. *Postcolonial Love Poem* by Natalie Diaz
   b. *Sana, Sana: Latinx Pain and Radical Visions for Healing and Justice*, edited by David Luis Glisch-Sánchez and Nic Rodriguez-Villafañe
   c. *The Pain We Carry: Healing from Complex PTSD for People of Color* by Natalie Y. Gutiérrez
   d. *My Mother Was a Freedom Fighter* by Aja Monet
   e. *Teaching About Gender Diversity: Teacher-Tested Lesson Plans for K-12 Classrooms*, edited by Susan W. Woolley and Lee Airton
4. Recommended Social Media Accounts:
   a. Therapy for Latinx: @therapyforlatinx
   b. Latinx Therapists Network: @latinxtherapy
   c. Genesis Espinoza, M.A., LMFT: @healing_and_growth
   d. Stephanie Ann Villaseñor, LMFT: @villasenorcounseling

LESSON SEQUENCE OVERVIEW AND STUDENT TEXT SET
Estamos bien: Talking Mental Health and Breaking Stigmas

Lesson #1	Lesson #2	Lesson #3	Lesson #4
"The Kids Are Not Alright: The Mental Health Crisis Affecting Latina Teens" video GLSEN National School Climate Survey	*The Carrying* and *The Hurting Kind* by Ada Limón "To Be Made Whole" *On Being* podcast episode (features poems from *The Carrying* and *The Hurting Kind*) *The Pain We Carry: Healing from Complex PTSD for People of Color* by Natalie Y. Gutiérrez	*Iveliz Explains It All* by Andrea Beatriz Arango *The Horn Book Magazine* "Publishers' Preview: Debut Authors: Five Questions for Andrea Beatriz Arango" Latinx KidLit Book Festival "How Do Writers Use Poetry to Tell a Story with Andrea Beatriz Arango" video Follet Learning "First Chapter Friday: *Iveliz Explains It All* by Andrea Beatriz Arango" video	*The Making of Yolanda La Bruja* by Lorraine Avila "Lorraine Avila Talks Being an Author and Using Her Voice to Stand Up for Issues in Her Community" *Growing Up Latina* podcast episode video "Lorraine Avila's Debut Novel Explores Brujería, Afro-Latina Girlhood, and Community" by Sofía Aguilar for *Hip Latina* website

Lesson #1: Talking Mental Health and Breaking Stigmas: A Multimodal Introduction

I was a middle-grade English teacher and dean at an independent school in New York State, where my office would be one of the spaces for processing middle-school life and restoration of friendships. Whether it was one of the Latina eighth graders who was discouraged by feedback on her writing in her English class or the lack of acknowledgement of Spanish language varieties in her Spanish class, I was always grateful for the trust we built and the many spaces students had to find support (middle-grade counselor's office, upper-school affinity groups). At one point, when someone had written an anti-LGBTQIA+ slur on a communal bench at the school, one of my students lamented, "We shouldn't have to wait until June." We were hurting. For weeks, queer students comforted each other and thought of creative ways to respond to the school community and administration. With support from thoughtful and kind staff, including the middle-grade counselor and high school Gender-Sexuality Alliance, the students decided to repaint the bench (see Figure 3.1). Although I was often with them as they raised concerns about a teacher's response to one of their requests to honor their pronouns or the lack of queer voices represented in the literature they read at school, I knew that this was one of many spaces and that I was one of several adults in their lives that they would need to help them feel like they truly belonged.

Middle school is a difficult time for a young person's development (especially growing up with online spaces that can inform so much of a young person's sense of self), and we must find ways for institutions to do right by this student group. I'm grateful that my middle-grade administration had weekly meetings with our counselor. I felt like those gatherings helped us revisit our support plans. Do all students feel like they truly belong in this space? Which student populations are most vulnerable at our school? How can we support them? What do we need to improve so that the entire school population can be in solidarity?

My year with these seventh and eighth graders taught me a lot about belonging and the role of institutions and community spaces in youth's well-being. It's never enough for students to feel acknowledged only for a day or a month (heritage months, Pride month). Also, acknowledgement or tolerance shouldn't be the goal. If we truly care about our students, especially our most vulnerable populations, we must actively find ways to live that in our school policies and practices.

FIGURE 3.1
Repainted bench

WRITING LESSON #1

LESSON TEXTS

- "The Kids Are Not Alright: The Mental Health Crisis Affecting Latina Teens" video (Vice, 2020)
- GLSEN National School Climate Survey

OBJECTIVES

Discussion: Discuss the factors contributing to the mental health crisis affecting Latinx teens.

Text Analysis: Explain how personal stories help us understand data (statistics, survey results).

Writing: Use primary sources to create an action plan to support students' well-being at school.

OPENING DISCUSSION

Show the Vice video "The Kids Are Not Alright: The Mental Health Crisis Affecting Latina Teens" (2020) and discuss the experiences of Latina teens. What do we learn about the different factors affecting Latina teens' health?

TEXT ANALYSIS

1. Compare the stories and expert quotes from "The Kids Are Not Alright: The Mental Health Crisis Affecting Latina Teens" video with the most recent data shared from the CDC Youth Risk Behavior Survey results. How does the video help us understand that data? In other words, how do stories help us get a better understanding of those numbers explaining rates of stress, anxiety, and depression in young people?
2. Look at the results of the latest GLSEN National School Climate Survey (NSCS) or your state's specific school climate survey ("State Snapshot"). GLSEN is a "multiracial, intergenerational LGBTQIA+ organization" that works with schools in the United States, providing resources for advocacy across educational institutions and movements (GLSEN, n.d.). How does the National School Climate Survey or the State Snapshot help us learn about the anti-LGBTQIA+ remarks heard in schools and their impact on the mental and physical health of young people in those schools?

WRITING

Invite students to consider the ways their school can help them navigate their lives. Students can use this opportunity to create a plan that addresses the following questions or support at their school:

1. Where can a student go for help in their school if they feel threatened or unsafe?
2. How can our school welcome students joining us at different points in the school year?
3. What more do we need to learn about populations of students who may be joining our school due to instability in their countries, changes in their home communities, or other obstacles?
4. Who makes up our counseling staff?
5. How can students set up appointments to see our counseling staff?
6. Who makes up our welcoming staff for newcomer students?
7. How can families and new students request support (staff, apps, online appointment platforms)?
8. Other: What other questions would be helpful to add to a document for new families/students?

It may be helpful to look at sample school websites for ways schools can make this information available to families and students. For example, the New York City East Side Community High School website links to the Counseling Office with student resources, parent resources, and even a virtual calming room with videos! If I were a parent of a child at this school, I could find answers to the questions above on that website and more.

CLOSING DISCUSSION

Examine the organizations that help youth take an active role in talking about their mental health and in partnering with communities. For example, youth in the area where I teach (New York City) have access to the following organizations (which also include resources on their websites):

- Girls for Gender Equity
- The Brotherhood Sister Sol
- Youth Advocacy Corps Mental Health Awareness Project

What are your local organizations (or national ones) that center youth voices to support mental health? Notice the images, media, and types of writing on those websites. Do they have blog posts written by young people? What do their policy briefs say? How do they present information to the general public in their press releases? What do these examples make you think about the role of writing for advocacy?

Lesson #2: Talking Mental Health and Breaking Stigmas: Poetry

There are several ways teacher preparation programs prepare you for the classroom, yet there are those moments in your teaching life where you'll say, "nothing could've prepared me for this!" I feel like those moments always happened to me, and I had some amazing professors, mentors, workshops, and classes. Of course, there are extreme times when students are impacted by world events or local and national government policies that affect them. However, what was most common in my classroom was supporting newcomer students who arrived at different points in the school year.

Mariano was one of them. Although he joined us at Don Pedro Albizu Campos School in the fall, he left before winter break. He was quiet, kept to himself for partner and group tasks, got by making sure he stayed off all teachers' radars (art, gym, social studies, science), and gradually started missing class—a lot. When I reached out to his grandmother to ask about him, she said he had to return to the Dominican Republic because it got to the point that he was no longer eating or engaging with anyone. He missed his parents dearly. They didn't have the required paperwork to travel with him. He felt alone, and it all became too much for him as a twelve-year-old.

What does it feel like to be seen? How could we have done better as a school community so Mariano could feel truly welcomed? In this lesson, we begin by exploring poetry as a way to truly see one another—something the twenty-fourth U.S. Poet Laureate Ada Limón describes as the power we have to witness the world while the world is witnessing us (2023). The human experience for people most impacted by inhumane policies (regarding immigration, healthcare, housing, climate change, and education) might be ignored or forgotten if we are not careful in being informed and in growing our advocacy. Mariano's departure heightened our senses, broke and expanded our hearts, and strengthened our class bonds with our families, school counselors, and other supportive adults.

WRITING LESSON #2

LESSON TEXTS

- *The Carrying* (2021) and *The Hurting Kind* (2022) by Ada Limón
- "To Be Made Whole" *On Being* podcast episode (Tippett, 2023) (features poems from *The Carrying* and *The Hurting Kind*)
- *The Pain We Carry: Healing from Complex PTSD for People of Color* by Natalie Y. Gutiérrez (2022)

OBJECTIVES

Discussion: Compare our experiences reading and writing poetry.

Text Analysis: Identify the use of sensory language to create parallels to human emotions.

Writing: Write a poem using the "borrowing a line" strategy inspired by "Sanctuary" or "After the Fire" by Ada Limón.

OPENING DISCUSSION

Ask students what their experiences have been with reading and writing poetry. How do they feel when they read poetry? How do they feel when they write poetry? Are there similarities or differences?

Share the following quote by poet Ada Limón from the *On Being* podcast with host Krista Tippett:

> And we read naturally for meaning. I mean, that's how we read. We read for sense. And poetry doesn't really allow you to do that because it's working in the smallest units of sound and syllable and clause and line break and then the sentence. So you get to have this experience with language that feels somewhat disjointed, and in that way almost feels like, "Oh, this makes more sense as the language for our human experience than, let's say, a news report."
>
> (Tippett, 2023, 13:04)

Have students discuss what they understand from this quote and whether they agree. It helps to know what students are bringing to their poetry workshops in the classroom (some bring trepidation because of prior schooling that focused on poetry as a to-do list instead of as a lens to view the world, while others bring excitement because in the past they've been encouraged to read and write poetry).

TEXT ANALYSIS

Option #1: "Sanctuary" from *The Hurting Kind* (2022) (also read on the *On Being* podcast episode with Ada Limón)

Option #2: "After the Fire" from *The Carrying* (2021) (also read on the *On Being* podcast episode with Ada Limón)

Read the poem as a class and then provide time for students to engage with it as a group or in partnerships. Have them annotate and read it out loud. Annotations can include instances where nature is referenced (a recurring theme in Ada Limón's poetry). If you haven't shared an annotation guide, tool, or graphic with the class, this is a great way to create one together (my preference). Using what they know about reading poetry from other classes or texts, what would they find important to annotate? Why? How would those notes help us understand the poem better? How do these annotations help us as writers? For example, my annotation for "After the Fire" might include underlining the similes and writing marginal notes about how the poem is an extended simile, with a focus on how Limón doesn't stop at a word for the comparison but elaborates with vivid imagery.

WRITING

Although these are brief lines from the poems to inspire our writing, the goals are to allow students to express themselves about our study topic and see poetry as another way they can breathe and exist in the world. Hopefully, they will feel moved to continue writing!

Option #1: Borrowing a line (or two) from "Sanctuary"

Use the last three lines about being made whole to inspire writing.
What do we need to be made whole? What do we need to feel at peace with our mind, spirit, and body?

Option #2: Borrowing a line (or two) from "After the Fire"

"You ever think you could [describe personal action here that shows an emotion] like [parallel action in nature] ... Funny thing about [emotion], [description of emotion], [simile connecting that description of the emotion with something else in the world]."

CLOSING DISCUSSION

Read the introduction to Natalie Y. Gutiérrez's *The Pain We Carry: Healing from Complex PTSD for People of Color* (2022):

> Dear Survivor. Let's start this conversation with a reminder: YOU are a resilient soul. If you've never been told this, I'm so glad you're here so I can tell you. I have so much gratitude for you, and your openness, as we begin this healing journey together. I want to say that I know some of you might be so tired of being resilient. That resilience has felt exhausting, that having to be strong has depleted many of your inner resources, and what you truly wish for is peace and safety.

Discuss how this relates to your life, writing, and other readings. Gutiérrez ends each chapter with some applications or what she calls empowerment steps: ways to use your body for self-regulation, addressing shame with self-compassion, bringing in ancestors' wisdom, and using tools that acknowledge an unjust system (2022). What are some of your next steps? Who are the people that can support you with this?

Lesson #3: Talking Mental Health and Breaking Stigmas: Middle-Grade Fiction

People often bristle at the mention of "middle school" or "I taught middle grade." Middle-grade teachers know what I'm talking about! This sense of dread comes over their faces, and I'm used to responding to that with my love for the middle graders' sense of curiosity, determination, and change. I'm grateful that I've had some thoughtful schools that have shown me creative ways to truly be there for our young people during this time in their lives.

De La Salle Academy (DLSA) is a unique independent school in the middle of Times Square, New York City, offering a small educational setting for low-income students. This school has shown me a healthy model of nurturing communication with middle-grade students, their families, and their teachers. I first learned of this school's mission when my husband was teaching there, and I often heard about their small group discussions across advisory sessions and how these helped sustain their sense of community (González, 2020). I worked with DLSA teachers and learned so much from their students during my time there (over three summers of teaching English, for two of which I directed the summer program). What caught my attention was how the staff intentionally saw the whole child and how the students were aware of their voices and brilliance. I was with them during very vulnerable times during the Black Lives Matter protests in the summer of 2020 and the global COVID-19 pandemic.

Not only were these young people grappling with their changing bodies, emotions, friendships, and academics (that transition from elementary to middle is a lot), but they were also grieving. They grieved the childhood they lost due to the pandemic shutdown, the family members they lost to COVID-19, and the Black lives lost and remembered as they witnessed the protests calling for justice. We read poetry, novels in verse, memoirs, fantasy, realistic fiction, and basically any texts that could engage them when everything seemed too much. There was too much change and unpredictability, and we were all trying to take it one breath, one day at a time.

Our writing together over those pandemic summers included community poems, personal narratives, reading responses, and fan fiction. Our favorite was capturing lines from our solar circle poems inspired by Juan Felipe Herrera's

"Social Distancing" (2020) poem. For our writing celebrations, some students created playlists for their characters, and some performed their poems. In contrast, others showed us other creative talents, such as self-portraits or graphic novel renderings of their writing. Of course, our virtual celebrations of these writing pieces couldn't come close to the in-person end-of-summer program gathering we had in 2018 but just having that space to be, to speak, to write, to breathe together was the healing I didn't know I needed during that time of so much loss.

Author Andrea Beatriz Arango's middle-grade novel in verse, *Iveliz Explains It All* (2023), captures that middle-grade voice, the power in communicating our feelings, and the community of support we should provide students for their mental health.

WRITING LESSON #3

LESSON TEXTS

- *Iveliz Explains It All* by Andrea Beatriz Arango (2022)
- *The Horn Book Magazine* "Publishers' Preview: Debut Authors: Five Questions for Andrea Beatriz Arango" (Sutton, 2022)
- Latinx KidLit Book Festival "How Do Writers Use Poetry to Tell a Story? With Andrea Beatriz Arango" video (2022)
- Follet Learning "First Chapter Friday: *Iveliz Explains It All* by Andrea Beatriz Arango" video (2022)

OBJECTIVES

Discussion: Explain the ways writers use poetry to tell a story.

Text Analysis: Identify how an author introduces a character, a problem, and feelings in a novel in verse.

Writing: Create a fictional character, problem, and feeling to set up a story using Andrea Beatriz Arango's recommended poetic devices (rhyme, repetition, varying sentence length).

OPENING DISCUSSION

See how author Andrea Beatriz Arango breaks down "Second Chances," the first poem in her novel in verse, *Iveliz Explains It All* (2022), in the Latinx KidLit Book

Festival video "How Do Writers Use Poetry To Tell a Story? With Andrea Beatriz Arango" (2022). How are the techniques Arango used different or similar to other types of writing? Do they resemble what you do as a writer?

TEXT ANALYSIS

Discuss this first poem as a class. As author Andrea Beatriz Arango tells us in the Latinx KidLit Book Festival video, Iveliz goes through a lot before we meet her in the first poem in the book. How do we know? In "Second Chances," we begin questioning what the first chance was, why Iveliz is in the principal's office, why she feels she can't ask anyone for help, and what happened that has her thinking she moved on from it so that seventh grade will be different. We also notice the impact that the repetition has on us ("love" in the first stanza, "I've" in the second stanza). It helps us understand how this character feels (like she's over it, confident she's got this).

WRITING

In the poem "Metí la pata," Iveliz writes the following in her journal:

But me? I'm always up and down
like a buttered bag of popcorn.
Sometimes unpopped.
Sometimes burnt to a crisp.
Almost never just right.
The medicine I take every day helps,
sort of (?),
or maybe it's just that I've gotten
    over all of **that**,
so anyways it's still useful,
de vez en cuando,
to just say something and see how
    Amir reacts.

When we've said too much, in English, we say, "stuck my foot in my mouth." In Spanish, some of us say "metí la pata." I chuckled when I read this poem's title (and in several parts of this heartbreaking yet heartwarming book). It's the first time I've seen this phrase as a title for a poem. By this point in the book, we know more about Iveliz's relationships (with her family, friends, teachers, and therapists), and here, with a comparison to popcorn, we learn more about the type of person Iveliz is.

This simile is an impactful reminder of how we can develop characters (or get to know ourselves even better) through comparisons. We can try this by thinking of a character we are developing in a story (if we are in a fiction-writing unit) or a real person (could be someone we know deeply or ourselves). In this example, the comparison works because Iveliz thinks about her feelings or how she navigates her life, capturing her emotions running high and low and never feeling just right using the image of popcorn kernels. We could borrow that framing of "I'm always ______ like ______. Sometimes ______, sometimes ______." What do we come up with in our writing? How do these similes work to reveal more about our characters, the people in our lives, or how we approach our lives?

CLOSING DISCUSSION

Option #1: Read *The Horn Book Magazine* "Publishers' Preview: Debut Authors: Five Questions for Andrea Beatriz Arango" (Sutton, 2022).

Students can read this short interview with author Andrea Beatriz Arango to learn about the reasons behind the author's decisions (developing a character grappling with pain and grief, use of English and Spanish, novel in verse form) and her teaching life. Students can discuss points of connection and how the book preview and interview might help them with their questions on mental health.

Option #2: Follet Learning "First Chapter Friday: *Iveliz Explains It All* by Andrea Beatriz Arango" video (2022)

Andrea Beatriz Arango reads several poems from the beginning of her book. How do these poems help readers understand the protagonist, her relationship with other people (her mother and grandmother, Mimi), and the issues she grapples with?

Lesson #4: Talking Mental Health and Breaking Stigmas: Young Adult Realistic Fiction

In the *Growing Up Latina* podcast, Black Dominican author Lorraine Avila shared that her writing and life's mission is to "rupture the tradition of silence that we have as a culture" (V, 2023, 49:10). We've seen across these texts in these lessons how common it is for some families and communities to completely ignore matters dealing with mental health. As countless generations before us have, we ignore the signs of distress or push deep feelings further and further down, continuing with our daily routines. This is so ingrained that many of us may not even have the language to express what it is that triggers our anxiety, or other ways our mind processes the ways we navigate the world.

Remember Sara, the undergraduate student in Childhood Education with a Bilingual Extension from the introduction to this chapter? I was taking the 2 train from the first stop at Brooklyn College Flatbush Avenue with Sara one day after class. She was commuting to the Bronx, and I was going to Westchester. Needless to say, we both had long commutes and could use the time to chat about life and our class. Our conversation started with the path toward securing an Individualized Education Program (IEP). Sara was holding it down for her family, attending all the meetings, translating at every meeting, and being the voice for her brother when he needed support for his mental health as well. In the midst of this constant advocacy, Sara was also the disruptor in her family, addressing machismo, domestic abuse, and the patriarchy; all the while, she was just trying her best to get through her undergraduate coursework and school fieldwork hours to prepare for student teaching. But you wouldn't have known any of this if you didn't specifically ask her to talk about it. And, even then, you might not get the full story. At one point in our journey, another commuter sitting across from us says, "excuse me, but this all sounds exhausting!" We laughed, maybe because we didn't want to cry, and the commuter proceeded to share his experiences with the school system, the decisions he made for the best place for his child's schooling, and he wished us good luck with our respective IEP processes.

I think a lot about Sara and the other undergraduate students I teach at Brooklyn College. They were high school students when the world shut down during the COVID-19 pandemic. Like my middle-grade students, they were well aware of the Black Lives Matter protests in our city, and while I write this book, they're witnessing genocide and multiple injustices at almost every turn in their social media engagement. Lorraine Avila's *The Making of Yolanda La Bruja* (2023) introduces us to a teen who grapples with listening to her spiritual guides and leaning into the reality of her many emotions while going to high school at a time when school shootings are an all-too-common occurrence. Avila says the following about her protagonist, Yolanda: "she is someone who deeply believes in herself, in her community, and in her powers as a person and as a bruja" (Aguilar, 2023). I hope that youth will find that same confidence in themselves and their community, especially during difficult times.

WRITING LESSON #4

LESSON TEXTS

- *The Making of Yolanda La Bruja* (2023) by Lorraine Avila
- "Lorraine Avila Talks Being an Author and Using Her Voice to Stand Up for Issues in Her Community" *Growing Up Latina* podcast episode video (V, 2023)
- "Lorraine Avila's Debut Novel Explores Brujería, Afro-Latina Girlhood, and Community" by Sofía Aguilar (2023) for *Hip Latina* website

OBJECTIVES

Discussion: Identify the spaces and people who support us in tough times.

Text Analysis: Track a character's relationship to people in different communities.

Writing: Consider different writing formats (journal entry, meditation, community norms) to expand on deep feelings.

OPENING DISCUSSION

Lorraine Avila on the *Growing Up Latina* episode

Students can discuss Lorraine Avila's writing journey (first five minutes of the episode) and points of connection. How does her writing journey mirror your own? What is different about Lorraine Avila's relationship to writing compared to your own? Why?

TEXT ANALYSIS

Yolanda is a Black Dominican American, queer, deaf teen. Share observations on different scenes that show how the protagonist connects with different communities that shape her well-being.

1. Discuss what we learn about the character in these scenes: Who does Yolanda feel safe with, and why? How does she communicate in these spaces?
2. Discuss what we learn about author Lorraine Avila's writing craft in these scenes: how does Lorraine Avila use dialogue, revealing actions, and narration (or internal dialogue) to reveal more about the themes of spirituality, community, and mental health?

Excerpt #1: Yolanda connecting with the spiritual realm, her "Bruja Diosas"

"After cleaning the energy, I start off with a little prayer," I look at Victory. "It can be anything you want, and to whomever or whatever you believe in." I close my eyes again. "Thank you Bruja Diosas, Guardian Angels, Goddesses, Gods, good-hearted Ancestros, Unknowns, Universe, and all that is wiser and greater than humans, for another day of life in this body and for the messages you will deliver." (p. 3)

Excerpt #2: Yolanda describes why it's not safe for Black and Brown people

It's a heavy time right now. Black and Brown folks being killed or harmed by a racist person, or police—at the supermarket, at a festival, in a church, at the movies. Plus, I saw on CNN that so far this year there has been at least one school shooting per week. It makes perfect sense that it feels like there is nowhere we can go to be fully safe anymore. (p. 7)

Excerpt #3: Yolanda connecting with friends and teacher in the Brave Space Club at school

I started the club in seventh grade with Victory's help, as always. Also our seventh grade ELA teacher, Ms. VanNorden, who sponsored the club. It was right after when we'd learned who the forty-fifth president of this country would be, someone who has proven to be hateful and honestly racist. But he showed to the world that there are more of them than many of us cooped up in big cities thought. After we moved to Julia De Burgos, Ms. VanNorden heard I was having a hard time in high school, and she connected with Mrs. Obi to bring the club here. (p. 98)

Excerpt #4: Yolanda connecting with her therapist

"Sweet Yoyo, you had a series of panic attacks. Fear, confusion, mental and emotional pressure—married to the negative energy of others around us—can definitely cause them. I don't know what your guides are trying to communicate, but I wouldn't discredit them. What I will say is our people have survived due to our spiritual connections. I am not sure it is time to give up on your Bruja Diosas yet."

I take a deep breath. Jonah is the first person I have ever talked to directly about my Bruja Diosas, other than Victory, Mamá Teté, and somewhat my parents. Mami always tells me to exaggerate about being sick to doctors, and never say too much to people about what I see and hear. Will I be a study case? Will I be locked away, examined, and probed? Suddenly I start feeling as if Jonah can see right through me. I bury my fists in the space between my thighs. I bring my shoulders in, and tuck my head onto my chest. I feel my cheeks flushing and then my ears are hot. *Take a deep breath. We're here. All is well. We're here. We haven't ever left your side.* (p. 293)

WRITING

Building on the previous lesson, Yolanda, like Iveliz, has ways of communicating their feelings. In *Iveliz Explains It All* (Arango, 2022), Iveliz se desahoga or let's it all out in her journal. Sometimes, she shares a few things with her best friend but, at first, doesn't open up completely with those around her. In *The Making of Yolanda La Bruja* (Avila, 2023), Yolanda has three spaces that hold space for her: her spiritual connection/community, the Brave Space Club at school, and therapy. Students can use this writing time to decide which will hold space for them:

- A journal entry like Iveliz: Write a personal journal entry on a strong emotion you have been feeling lately. List the moments that triggered that emotion. Select one and write what you remember from that moment using different senses.
- A prayer or meditation like Yolanda's: Write a prayer that expresses something in your heart at this moment and what you'd like to feel or make space for in the future. Some prayers are said to beings that form part of someone's spiritual practices. Other prayers, like the one described by host of the *Growing*

Up Latina podcast, Alyi V (on the episode with Lorraine Avila), can be to your future self.

- A community space like The Brave Space Club that Yolanda started: What would a space like this look like, feel like, or sound like at your school (if it doesn't exist already)? Design your Brave Space Club group norms or mission statement. What would be the purpose of your gatherings? Who is welcome? What would you discuss? How would you hold space for students in your school?

CLOSING DISCUSSION

Read "Lorraine Avila's Debut Novel Explores Brujería, Afro-Latina Girlhood, and Community" by Sofía Aguilar (2023) on *Hip Latina*. Discuss the path to publication and author Lorraine Avila's challenges (publishers wanting scenes removed and Black Dominican Spanish changed). Avila shares the following about Yolanda, the protagonist:

"She's surrounded by a community that allows her to be imperfect," Avila says. "Our communities are always telling us that we have to be four times as best, as good as the person next to us, that we have to be on our best behavior, that we have to think about respectability politics if we want to have success in any area of our life. But Yolanda's allowed to make mistakes. I also love that she is someone who deeply believes in herself, in her community, and in her powers as a person and as a bruja. She's shaken by the things going on around her but she's not really doubting herself. She questions things in certain moments, but she doesn't doubt that this is all leading to the best version of herself possible."

Students can discuss whether this has been their experience. Have they felt the pressure to be perfect at all times? Are they allowed to make mistakes? How do they feel about those moments of lapse in judgment? How can they come out of those moments, hoping that this is all "leading to the best version" of themselves?

TESTIMONIO: Raúl Vaquero

High School Global Literature Teacher, Immigrant Liaison, and DACA Student Club Teacher, New York City Public Schools

Raúl was one of my graduate students in the TESOL program at Bank Street Graduate School of Education. His advocacy and teaching of writing with bilingual and multilingual students is a helpful example for educators seeking ways to connect with their students through writing while also nurturing their own writing practice.

RAÚL ON HIS JOURNEY AS AN EDUCATOR:

It is truly a labor of love that takes and gives back in ways I would never expect. I started teaching ENL [English as a New Language] at the International High School [at] Union Square. The course class, however, is titled Global Literature. And the logic behind it was rather mysterious to me, so I'm adding my own interpretation to it. Decentering the English language and places and then focusing on the acquisition of the English language through literature from a global lens. And I started teaching three years ago and continue with the same role. However, over the past three years, my role has evolved from designing curriculum to being my school's immigrant liaison, cofacilitating clubs like Dream Team and Alianza, to being Dream Team leader this year. Through these roles, I found myself steeped in deep reflection and with an intense desire to do better every day and fully embrace the positive and negative spontaneity that comes with being an educator because some days being an educator is full of celebration, happiness, healing and justice for oneself and humanity and other days it's riddled with exhaustion, teen angst, systemic and global turmoil. It also applies to doing a better job taking care of myself in a way that makes the line of work that we do sustainable.

RAÚL ON HIS FIRST MEMORY OF SEEING HIMSELF AS A WRITER:

The first time I saw myself as a writer was in my sophomore year of high school. At the time, I didn't really know what it meant to be one. All I understood was the act itself and that only güeritos could enjoy and indulge. However, all of that changed after a couple of creative assignments. Each playful piece that I created fueled my desire to understand what it means to be a writer because after completing each piece I continued to feel awkward and empty. So I sought out inspiration that led me to Barnes and Noble close by my high school. But nothing caught my attention. After a certain point, I started turning to the literary canon, for answers about what it means to be a writer to write exceptionally well and be well-read. And this journey led me into several Eurocentric rabbit holes. Somehow, I got introduced later to the works of Malcolm X, Huey Newton, Maya Angelou, Gloria Anzaldúa, Rodolfo "Corky" Gonzales, and many like-minded authors that provided me the opportunity to finally see myself in the literature. And to understand that to be a writer means understanding what language can do, and once that's acquired, one wields the ability to make others feel through harnessing the power of the word. It's thanks to them that I was finally able to see myself as a writer.

RAÚL ON HIS FAVORITE WRITING ACTIVITY WITH LATINX TEENS:

I think my favorite writing activity with Latinx teens is something that runs closely for me, which is introspective writing because it encourages people to write without worrying about whether or not it's grammatically correct. It allows one to write freely and develop their self-awareness about the world around them. I think if you can't understand yourself, you can't really understand others. That's my favorite activity and quite often our culture denies or limits that self-reflection, self-reflexivity that promotes so much growth.

RAÚL ON LATINX AUTHORS GIVING HIM LIFE RIGHT NOW:

Aida Salazar with *Land of the Cranes* and *A Seed in the Sun*. Also, Alexandra Villasante's *The Grief Keeper*. Especially right now, in the line of work that I do as one of the facilitators of the Dream Team club, where we focus primarily on teaching students about their rights as immigrants.

RAÚL'S ADVICE FOR WRITING TEACHERS OF LATINX YOUTH:

Stray away from the mechanics of writing. Allow students to express themselves in whatever modality they prefer, and never accept the bare minimum. I think that's one thing that I learned but also contend with because teaching writing demands that one is trauma-informed, and I think that's one area that I'm not well-versed in, and I sometimes tread carefully when it comes to not accepting the bare minimum because I lack that lens. Tread carefully and focus on creating the space for students to freely express themselves.

WRITING THAT RAÚL IS WORKING ON RIGHT NOW:

Right now, I'm working on writing every day, and I'm using *The Artist's Way* by Julia Cameron's morning pages. It's helping me with this illusion of writer's block and reframe how I approach writing. I think I was seeing it more as a thing of producing instead of a thing of creating. That distinction was very hard for me to process. The other thing that I'm working on is an autoethnography.

Chapter Four

Learning a New Language, Learning a New Me

"Yo me inspiré a escribir cuando yo vine de Santo Domingo a los Estados Unidos porque en ese momento yo no sabía que escribir pero yo me recordé como yo extraño a mi mamá, yo podía escribir eso ... uno nunca se tiene que dar por vencido ... y también que nunca deje su cultura y uno tiene que escribir los dos idiomas si uno le parece ... uno siempre tiene que escribir inglés y español para tener un mejor futuro ... Me imagino en ese momento yo estoy como llena de felicidad ... veo que las personas cuando ellos necesitan ayuda uno lo tiene que ayudar."

—Ana, sixth-grade student (España, 2017, p. 192)

Ana and her sister Oscary, participants in my middle-grade writing research study (España, 2017), had a common experience with those who speak languages other than English and started school in a monolingual English program. Upon arriving from the Dominican Republic during upper elementary school, they were placed at computers for most of their day to "learn English." Yet this is not what we gather from the opening quote! Ana describes a joy and freedom with writing, especially with that realization that she could write about how much she missed her mom, who remained in the Dominican Republic, a common practice for immigrant families who are separated when documentation is not granted for everyone to remain together. This drastic difference can be credited to her experiences in her new school, specifically her sixth-grade English as a New Language (ENL) writing class. In this opening quote, we also read her advice for newcomers to "write in both languages" for a "better future," and when I asked her how she sees herself in the future doing this, she said, "full of happiness ... seeing people who need help and one has to help them" (España, 2017). The sense of confidence as a writer and responsibility as a bilingual speaker reverberated through all of my interviews with Ana and her classmates. But it wasn't sitting at a computer learning English from a program that contributed to this transformation. Ana says her current middle-grade teacher is better at teaching English because Ana now learns writing strategies and is encouraged to use her Spanish and English (España, 2017).

How are schools supported to welcome and encourage students who are learning English? While some schools have Dual Language Bilingual Education, Transitional Bilingual, and English as a New Language classes, others may not have these types of supports. According to the National Center for Education Statistics, over five million students are labeled as "English learners" in public schools in the United States (2023). By 2025, one in every four students in the United States will be an "English language learner," or a bilingual or multilingual student learning English (National Education Association, 2020). To add another layer of concern and complexity, although some schools may have these types of programming, we must be cautious to discern who benefits from these classes and whether racialized language-minoritized children are encouraged in their bilingualism or are being used to support and celebrate the bilingual trajectory of white, English-dominant children (Flores & García, 2017), while their own is interpreted as deficient.

From those who make up the Latinx diaspora, we must also consider that Spanish is not the only language spoken by these students and their families. In this group, we must include Haitian Creole, Portuguese, Chinese, Arabic, and the many Indigenous languages spoken throughout the Americas. One year, when I was teaching a seventh-grade English as a New Language class, I had English,

Spanish, Arabic, and Mixtec speakers. Whether it is a Chilean Palestinian student who speaks Spanish and Arabic, a student from Peru speaking Quechua, or a newcomer from Oaxaca, Mexico, speaking Mixtec or Nahuatl, our emergent bilingual and multilingual students have the right to an education that acknowledges this part of their identity—see the United Nations Convention on the Rights of the Child Articles 29, 30, and 40 (United Nations, 1989). Many misconceptions or assumptions about students arriving from Latin America and the languages they speak can be dispelled if we reject the myth of the Latinx monolith (see Chapter 7) and challenge ourselves to learn more about these populations.

Ana's teacher, Ms. Medina, took up that challenge, learning more about her students from the Dominican Republic and Mexico. At first, when starting her teaching journey, her former principal told her not to speak Spanish to Spanish-speaking students. Ms. Medina followed that rule and would limit her Peruvian Spanish to conversations with families or students during recess. It took years for her to come to terms with her judgment about her students' Spanish, especially Caribbean Spanish. She began teaching from a place of privilege and assumptions that her Spanish from Peru was the correct one. When the City University of New York–New York State Initiative on Emergent Bilinguals (CUNY-NYSIEB) partnered with her school, offering professional learning opportunities for teaching bilingual learners to the (new) administration and teaching staff, Alejandra Medina's language ideologies shifted. She learned about translanguaging as an orientation to language, going beyond the named languages and the constrictions that can come with that perspective, instead moving towards an understanding that bilinguals and multilinguals use one language repertoire with many features from a variety of those "named languages," and they do so dynamically and in context with our social situations (García et al., 2021; Vogel & García, 2017). She learned about translanguaging as a teaching method, something she had already begun to do in her ENL classroom, which she was now finding validated by the latest research on translanguaging pedagogy (García & Kleyn, 2016; de los Ríos & Seltzer, 2017). So, students in her class, like Ana, felt nourished as bilingual writers, employing their many varieties of Spanish and English across narrative, argument, and informational writing units.

Ana's experience in Ms. Medina's classroom would've been much different had her teacher not faced her assumptions about Spanish language varieties from the Caribbean. This much-needed "aha" moment was a product of a commitment to collaboration and seeing the full humanity of all her students. What do we call these ideas about certain language practices from certain populations; more specifically, those people that are racialized or labeled as "minorities"? In an interview on *AnthroPod*, the podcast of the Society for Cultural Anthropology, linguistic-anthropologist scholar Dr. Jonathan Rosa shares the following (Bean, 2020):

> What interests me most about studying language patterns is the way that, again, minute features of language can become positioned as high stakes signals of belonging, of legitimacy, of intelligence, of personhood broadly construed. And so for me, the relevance of this conversation about raciolinguistic ideologies and language ideologies more broadly is sort of saying, wait a second, this is a lens into figuring out the kinds of worlds that we have constructed, where certain forms of personhood are legitimate and other forms of personhood are illegitimate ... And so for me, what look like casual jokes, casual commentary, casual recognition, are in fact mobilizing profound histories of colonialism, profound histories of racial capitalism, profound histories of patriarchy, profound histories of a set of ideas around ability and legitimate sort of capacity or one's capacity for thought, this sort of thing.

Not only had Ms. Medina experienced exactly what Dr. Rosa speaks of here, with her language practices interpreted as illegitimate (one of her New York University teacher preparation courses and student teaching experiences included disparaging comments on her accent and her decision to teach emergent bilingual students), but without noticing it, she had been doing the same, repeating that cycle with her students. In the summer of 2015, the Harvard Education Review journal published "Undoing Appropriateness: Raciolinguistic Ideologies and Language Diversity in Education" by Nelson Flores and Jonathan Rosa, and the fields of linguistics, bilingual education, TESOL education, and education policy will never be the same. This groundbreaking piece introduced us to the term Flores and Rosa coined, "raciolinguistic ideologies," something we've already been exposed to through the quotes from the children, undergraduate students, and teachers in my research across this book. Flores and Rosa use the phrase "raciolinguistic ideologies" to help us consider the following in our understanding of languages and the language-learning process; most specifically, how racialized speakers are viewed when they learn English: race and language are co-constructed, with race at the center of the analysis; English learners are viewed as deficient by those listeners who employ raciolinguistic ideologies discrediting and belittling the communication practices of racialized bilinguals; and there is a need to shift the focus from the student learning English to the listener who holds harmful ideas about these students (2015). Flores and Rosa also call our attention to these ideologies that are present in the "white listening subject," who can be a white monolingual speaker or a monolingual/bilingual person of color who has internalized this colonial mindset.

For example, do we celebrate white monolingual English-speaking children when they are enrolled in a bilingual dual language education class and begin to learn

Spanish but not do the same for the Latinx students in that same class who speak Spanish and are starting to learn English? Do we express the same type of awe and admiration with the Indigenous student from Oaxaca, Mexico, who speaks Nahuatl as we do with the white child who is learning Spanish? What about the English classes with French and Haitian Creole speakers from France and those from West Africa and Haiti? Do we celebrate all varieties of those languages? Whose language practices are welcomed in our writing community, and who is expected to assimilate into a monolingual English standard we set? I share these examples because these have all been children in schools I've taught at, consulted with on literacy curriculum development workshops, or connected with as a teacher educator through teacher education programs. Even for those of you who do not have any of these speakers represented in your classrooms and on your campuses, I would still encourage you to think of the representation of English and other languages in the literature you use to facilitate writing instruction.

It is with this reality and concern in mind that bilingual teacher educator Luz Yadira Herrera and I developed the Critical Bilingual Literacies Framework (España & Herrera, 2020), which encourages teachers to practice ongoing self-reflection on our language ideologies, engage in an analysis of language that includes issues of power and histories of colonialism, unlearn the harmful hierarchies of language that set up linguistic supremacy that favors white monolingual speakers, and celebrate bilingual and multilingual students' languages and identities. This chapter's sequence of lessons serves as a guide for students to engage in that unlearning and (re)learning on issues of language and identity so that they can grapple with the tensions and what it means to be a racialized bilingual or multilingual being in a society, community, or school that has been by default set up not to have space for them. These lessons help students take up that space with their ideas and writing.

My poem "ESL" grapples with my past and present tensions as a bilingual person and educator, continuously developing my English and Spanish. My introduction to English was when I began kindergarten in an English classroom in the United States. This was almost three decades before the school launched its bilingual dual language program in Spanish and Chinese. I had friends from different regions in Asia, the Caribbean, and the Americas. My Caribbean friends, Jeanette and Dana, helped translate for me, and my friend Ladika from Pakistan joined me in class assignments and performances. The two spaces that brought me the most joy at this time were the school library, and anywhere we had band practice. I would often get pulled out of my class for English as a Second Language (ESL) services, along with other students. We'd gather in a small room where we'd practice our English.

Poem: "ESL"

I forget the word for straw in
Chilean Spanish
and despite having lived here for
thirty-seven years,
I make an embarrassing and epic mistake:
I stand in the middle of Times Square,
tourists whizzing by,
so I can get on the family WhatsApp.

What a simple thing,
requests for a grandchild's packed lunch.
Sí, leche por favor con vaso y
sorbete/bombilla/straw
(se me olvidó cómo se dice en Chile 😭).

I'm five-years-old, back at PS 13 in Corona, Queens.
Sitting on the floor.
A small circle of us.
Newcomers.
Grammar sheets and workbooks.
Rules and conversations.
English growing like weeds
overpowering the blossoms of
Spanish.

I was told ESL was
English as a Second Language
but maybe a better description would be
English Suffocating Language (of Home).

How quickly we forget the names of simple things
we learn from the people who love us most.

Personal Narrative: "Saturday School: La Escuela Argentina"

I was in graduate school when I first learned the phrase "community cultural wealth" through scholar Tara J. Yosso's (2005) work. It helped me understand how my family navigated my introduction to monolingual English schooling in New York City. Our emerging NYC family, their networks, and our local Queens community were integral to our understanding of how to exist, learning a new language, and learning a new land (Suárez-Orozco, Suárez-Orozco, & Todorova, 2010). "Saturday School: La Escuela Argentina" is a response to the prompt I often give teen and young adult writers: *write a short personal narrative on one moment from your childhood that you understand more of now but were unaware of in the past.* I explain that the writing will be shared with students from lower grades to help them learn more about these times in our lives and the issues they engender. Although the piece is a response to that prompt, it's also a thank you to the friends (now family) who have played an integral role in my family's immigration journey. If it weren't for those neighbors-turned-friends-turned-family, it would have been very difficult and nearly impossible for my family to learn about different school options and ways to continue nurturing my bilingualism and connection to family over five thousand miles away.

"Que le vaya bien mi amor," tía Isabel waves as she closes the basement door behind her. She may be the "super's wife" to our neighbors, but for me, she's my tía, the first person we met when we came from Chile. She also walked us to the local public school and told us about a Saturday school in Spanish when we learned that the school did not have a bilingual program.

Mamá takes me to my English school on Mondays to Fridays, but Saturday mornings are my special time with papá. "¿Quieres practicar?" papá asks. La Escuela Argentina is five blocks away. I spend most of our walks singing and practicing my steps for the upcoming performance.

"¿Estás nerviosa? ¡No te preocupes! Te salió muy bien el baile anoche!"

When papá gets home from the restaurant, I love smelling his clothes. Fried empanadas and parilladas. I close my eyes and imagine I'm back at cerro Gómez Carreño with my abuelita in her kitchen. He'll ask me to share phrases in English that I learned during the day. We have our "English time." I teach him the little I know. My mom doesn't care for it. She prefers we share stories of our family, our days in my pre-school in Valparaíso and our fun performances with the Chilean folklore group. She's afraid I'll forget. I know this because, whenever we go to the dollar store, she gets me special pencils and paper. "Para que le escribas a la tía Marcela," she encourages me to write to my aunt and tell her what I'm learning.

Today, at La Escuela Argentina, we have our final rehearsal for "Celebraciones del pueblo."

"Creo que estás lista," says papá, giving me all the confidence I need to get on that stage and dance it out.

I want to tell papá that it's not that simple. I spend hours confused in school during the week. I want to be back home with our family, walking the craft fairs in Viña del Mar, running in the fields in Olmué with my cousins. But I don't want to complain. I don't understand this "we don't have the necessary papers" concern I keep hearing about. Why do we need a "special permission" to be with family?

Papá sees the skeptical look on my face. "Hoy practicamos en casa y le pedimos a la tía Isabel que nos ayude." What a great idea! Tía Isabel is from Argentina, knows this song, and her kids go to Escuela Argentina, too!

I think of the love surrounding me with family in Chile and the new family we are creating in New York. Like one of my favorite singers (from Argentina), Mercedes Sosa, says in "Todo cambia," even though everything changes and we may be far from our homelands, our love remains.

Performing at La Escuela Argentina in Queens, New York

TEACHER TEXT SET

1. Media: Podcasts
   a. The Society for Cultural Anthropology *AnthroPod* podcast "Raciolinguistic Ideologies and Decolonizing Anthropology: A Conversation with Jonathan Rosa"
   b. *Vocal Fries* podcast "Bilingualism Is. It Just Is"
   c. *Vocal Fries* podcast "Don't Mind the Gap"
2. Media: Videos
   a. "Translanguaging in 15 Minutes" by Mike Mena on *The Social Life of Language* YouTube channel

   b. "Ofelia García and Li Wei: Translanguaging: Language, Bilingualism, and Education (2014)" by Mike Mena on *The Social Life of Language* YouTube channel
   c. "Immersion" by Media that Matters
   d. Teacher-leader videos from Translanguaging Resources on the City University of New York–New York State Initiative on Emergent Bilinguals website (CUNY-NYSIEB, 2019)
   e. *Somos Escritoras* website
3. Articles:
   a. "Translating Theory to Practice: Exploring Teachers' Raciolinguistic Literacies in Secondary English Classrooms" by Kate Seltzer and Cati V. de los Ríos
   b. "Raciolinguistics and the Education of Emergent Bilinguals Labeled as Disabled" by María Cioè-Peña
   c. "From Academic Language to Language Architecture: Challenging Raciolinguistic Ideologies in Research and Practice" by Nelson Flores
   d. "Language" by Ofelia García in the *Wiley Blackwell Encyclopedia of Race, Ethnicity, and Nationalism*
   e. "Translanguaging" from the *Oxford Encyclopedia of Education* by Sara Vogel and Ofelia García
4. Policy briefs and handouts:
   a. "Understanding Translanguaging in US Literacy Classrooms: Reframing Bi-/Multilingualism as the Norm" by Kate Seltzer and Cati V. de los Ríos
   b. "What Anti-Racist Language Teachers Do" handout: NCTE Committee Against Racism and Bias in the Teaching of English (CARBTE Chair, Lorena Germán)
5. Books:
   a. *The Translanguaging Classroom: Leveraging Student Bilingualism for Learning* by Ofelia García, Susana Ibarra-Johnson, and Kate Seltzer
   b. *Daughters of Latin America: An International Anthology of Writing by Latine Women* edited by Sandra Guzmán
   c. *My Broken Language: A Memoir* by Quiara Alegría Hudes
   d. *Borderlands/ La Frontera: The New Mestiza* by Gloria Anzaldúa
   e. *Rooted in Strength: Using Translanguaging to Grow Multilingual Readers and Writers* by Cecilia M. Espinosa and Laura Ascenzi-Moreno

LESSON SEQUENCE OVERVIEW AND STUDENT TEXT SET Learning a New Language, Learning a New Me			
Lesson #1	**Lesson #2**	**Lesson #3**	**Lesson #4**
"Translanguaging in 15 Minutes" video by Dr. Mike Mena on *The Social Life of Language* YouTube channel	"Translation" by Yesika Salgado (spoken word performance) "Translation for Mamá" and "My Father in English" poems by Richard Blanco in *Homeland of My Body: New and Selected Poems*	*The Year I Flew Away* by Marie Arnold *We Need Diverse Books* blog "Marie Arnold Writes So Immigrant Readers Feel Seen" by Karis Rogerson	"Karla Sánchez and Yásnaya Elena Aguilar Gil" from *Daughters of Latin America: An International Anthology of Writing by Latine Women* edited by Sandra Guzmán

Lesson #1: Learning a New Language, Learning a New Me: A Multimodal Introduction

My child, Luna, loves all things music, movement, and books. As a child of a Chilean mother and Colombian father who grew up in New York City, Luna hears all kinds of words in Spanish and English. Although her schooling has been English dominant, she's immersed in Spanish at all family weekend gatherings with grandparents who shower her with love and, in typical grandparent fashion, often do not say no to her. Before her special-education evaluation conducted by bilingual Spanish-English educators, I had begun to keep a notebook of how Luna was developing language. As a bilingual educator and now mother, it was fascinating to see the way Luna described objects and people, how she expressed her feelings, and how she navigated the bilingual home life. It's been over a year since that evaluation and my lists of words and very short phrases. Now that I've been having lengthier conversations with Luna, I have a more personal connection to the bilingual and multilingual scenarios I was presented with in my teacher preparation programs on language development. I'm in constant awe at how Luna and other bi/multilingual children navigate their language practices.

Although learning about translanguaging was a powerful "aha" moment for Alejandra Medina, the Peruvian teacher from my research study that I describe in the introduction to this chapter, it is often either misunderstood or rejected by educators. I've been to several schools where either an administrator or a teacher shares that their supervisor has not allowed them to use translanguaging pedagogy or even to say the word translanguaging! When I was a literacy consultant, one superintendent in a New York City district was not open to any research on this and told their schools not to use it. I find that those of us within the bilingual and multilingual communities who pull from a vast repertoire of language resources and can shift across times and contexts completely understand the translanguaging orientation that does not see a border between languages. This "insider" view is crucial because often it is either outsiders (who are monolingual) or insiders (language-minoritized speakers) who attempt to be accepted by those outsiders who design curriculum, pedagogy, and policies for bilingual and multilingual speakers, dismissing the very real experiences of those students who are most impacted. Language and Race scholar Dr. Mike Mena's YouTube channel, *The Social Life of Language*, is a helpful resource to respond to this reality. The following lesson supports students as they process the "Translanguaging in 15 Minutes" video by Dr. Mike Mena (The Social Life of Language, 2020). Dr. Mena, a Mexican American researcher, is not only an expert in this field but is also my colleague in Puerto Rican and Latinx Studies. We sometimes teach the same students and I've had the privilege of seeing how our students carry over his teaching from one class to another. I'm most overjoyed when I see them connecting what they see at their school sites with what they're learning with Prof. Mena. I encourage you to check out *The Social Life of Language* YouTube channel!

WRITING LESSON #1

LESSON TEXT

"Translanguaging in 15 Minutes" video by Dr. Mike Mena (The Social Life of Language, 2020) on *The Social Life of Language* YouTube channel

OBJECTIVES

Discussion: Discuss the meaning of key words related to language and language learning.

Text Analysis: Analyze a text's central idea and supporting details.

Writing: Compose a short narrative that can be used as a case study/simulation scenario for teachers, administrators, and language policymakers to learn about translanguaging.

OPENING DISCUSSION

Provide students with a list of key words (we'll see these explained in the video) and ask them to identify which of these they've heard before, which they've heard before and can explain the meaning of, and which they've never heard before:

- Perspective
- Translanguaging
- Code-switching
- Language
- Colonizer

TEXT ANALYSIS

Follow this discussion guide to process the central idea and supporting details in the "Translanguaging in 15 Minutes" video on *The Social Life of Language* YouTube channel.

Part One [minutes 1:10–3:00]
Guiding Question from Prof. Mike Mena: How does a language get a name?

Part Two [minutes 3:00–5:05]
Guiding Question: Why would a colonizer or colonizing institution be interested in studying the colonized peoples' language practices?

Part Three [minutes 5:05–8:10]
Guiding Question: What does it mean that "a named language is a social construct"?

Part Four [minutes 8:10–10:00]
Guiding Question: What do we assume when discussing code-switching between named languages?

Part Five [minutes 10:00–12:15]
Guiding Question: Why can't we say translanguaging and code-switching are the same?

Part Six [minutes 12:15–14:00]
What example does Prof. Mike Mena give to explain the following quote? "Translanguaging is the deployment of a speaker's full linguistic repertoire without

regard for watchful adherence to the socially and politically defined boundaries of named (and usually national and state) languages" (p. 283 in Otheguy, García, and Reid, "Clarifying Translanguaging and Deconstructing Named Languages: A Perspective from Linguistics," 2015).

WRITING

Revisit the last two minutes of Prof. Mike Mena's video "Translanguaging in 15 Minutes." Consider creating a scenario that could be shared with school administrators, teachers, and language policymakers to explain the difference between a bilingual/multilingual child learning to speak at home and the changes they face when they enter a monolingual school setting or how their language repertoire develops.

For example, I share the process for my child, Luna, in the scenario below.

Scenario:

Luna is a four-year-old child with parents from Chile and Colombia. She grew up in a multigenerational home, with grandparents who spoke Spanish and parents who spoke both English and Spanish. She quickly became a fan of the *Ms. Rachel* videos, helping her name her feelings and develop vocabulary for several nouns in English. She watched *1, 2, 3 Andrés* and *Canticos* videos for bilingual Spanish-English songs. When she turned three, she became a fan of Disney films, obsessed over listening to the Spanish and English soundtracks and asked the family to join in the fun of performing the songs. During this period of her life (ages 3–4), Luna attended a school where English was the language of instruction but where several teachers spoke Spanish and would greet her and have conversations with her in Spanish. Some of Luna's favorite phrases sound like the following:

- "I had a great day in escuela today."
- "Gracias, mamá. Thank you, papa." (Luna says "papa" and not "papá.")
- "Can you play arts and crafts with me, mama?" (Luna says "mama," not "mamá.")
- "I want to go to bookstore."
- "Can you help me?"
- "I miss casita Luna."
- "Tengo hambre."

- "Leche por favor."
- "No quiero camita Luna."
- "How was school today, mama?" (Luna says "mama," not "mamá.")

In her first year in school, Luna had teachers who spoke English, Spanish, Korean, and Hungarian. One of the first songs she learned in school greeted the morning and the Earth, followed by one where they greeted each other in different languages.

CLOSING DISCUSSION

We usually focus craft discussions on texts like books, short stories, articles, poems, and personal narratives. Use this opportunity to discuss the craft that Prof. Mike Mena used in this video to explain these concepts and excerpts from that article. For example, guide students by asking:

- How did the video use lighting? What effect did it have?
- How did the video use audio? What effect did it have?
- How did Prof. Mike Mena discuss the content of the article? How did this approach impact you as a viewer?
- How did Prof. Mike Mena include different media (visuals and words) in the video? What effect did these have?

Extension/Bonus Question: What concept or text that the class has been studying would benefit from an explainer video like this? Encourage students to consider how and when they can work on a short video following Prof. Mike Mena's example.

Lesson #2: Learning a New Land, Learning a New Me: Poetry

Before I embarked on my teacher education journey, when I was completing graduate studies at Princeton Theological Seminary, I worked at Arm in Arm (formerly the Crisis Ministry of Mercer County), a non-profit in Trenton, New Jersey. There, I interacted with local families and was grateful I could use my bilingualism to provide information on support services and to learn more about the families' experiences. My time there changed my life as my assumptions were challenged, especially around equity and low-income communities (particularly with undocumented women of color). The conversations with families at Arm in Arm and liberating pedagogies graduate courses made me consider a career in bilingual education. I remember seeing children join me in translating information for their families and I saw my own childhood reflected in them.

When I taught middle-grade bilingual students, I was grateful I could communicate with their families and not place that responsibility on the children (although translation services were available in our district, these are often stretched thin). Although translating is often interpreted as something to take pride in, as children relish the opportunity to show their skills (as we've seen in the sixth graders' comments from my research that I've shared in the opening chapter quotes), it can also create much anxiety. This practice of language brokering (Faulstich Orellana, 2009; Tse, 1995) by immigrant children and children of immigrants who speak languages other than English is not only in service of their families but also of the "larger society, as they speak to and for doctors, teachers, store personnel, service providers, and more" (Faulstich Orellana, n.d.). The poetry by Yesika Salgado and Richard Blanco helps us think about translations and the act of translating. When something is difficult—as it can be when our existence embodies translation—I often turn to the poets.

WRITING LESSON #2

LESSON TEXTS

- "Translation" by Yesika Salgado (All Def Poetry, 2015) (spoken word performance)
- "Translation for Mamá" and "My Father in English" poems by Richard Blanco in *Homeland of My Body: New and Selected Poems* (2023)

OBJECTIVES

Discussion: Discuss what it means to translate something and what translations look like in our lives (for friends, family; for class assignments in a language course).

Text Analysis: Identify different poetry structures.

Writing: Try different poetry brainstorming prompts and strategies to write a "Translation for ______" poem.

OPENING DISCUSSION

What does it mean to translate? What gets lost in translation? How can translations be helpful? Consider these opening questions before showing students Salvadoran poet Yesika Salgado's performance of "Translation." Ask students to consider how the poem made them feel and what they learned about Salgado's relationship to her bilingualism (Spanish, English) and her mother.

TEXT ANALYSIS

Read "Translation for Mamá" by Richard Blanco (2023). Use the Poetry as Teaching, Resistance, and Healing Framework (see page 173; España & Herrera, 2020; Appendix B) to read the poem a few times and focus on what the poem teaches us, how it can be healing, and what it resists. Although the teacher may read the poem the first time, a second or third reading can have students in groups alternating the reading in English and Spanish.

- Poetry as Teaching: What do we learn about Blanco's family's connection to Cuba? What do we learn about what Blanco translates for his mamá? What do we learn about the structure of the poem?
- Poetry as Resistance: How can this poem's structure and content be a form of resistance to monolingualism (note how the entire poem is separated by language and Spanish is italicized and indented until the end)?
- Poetry as Healing: How does this poem help bilinguals and multilinguals, especially from language-minoritized populations (and/or people who are exiles), consider what they've gained and what they've lost in the transitions and translations of their lives?

WRITING

Consider asking students to write their own "Translation for ______" poem. They can use any of the following poetry brainstorming strategies for ideas:

- **Borrow a line:** Select one line and work from there to finish that sentence. For example, Blanco writes, "In English I have told you ..." and we can consider what we have said or written when translating for friends and family.

- **Repetition:** Return to what is repeated in Blanco's poem (for example, the line "in English") and consider whether you want to write a poem with that same line repeating or create a different phrase you'd repeat (example: "I translated at ..." or "I never quite knew if my translation was correct when ...).
- **Tell a story:** Recall a moment when translation was important for your friends or family: a class assignment, a doctor's visit, a phone call, etc. Tell the story of that moment using different senses as you remember how you felt, what you saw, what you said, and what others said and did during this scene. Write, write, write, and return to add line breaks to help give form to your poem (if necessary).

CLOSING DISCUSSION

Read "My Father in English" by Richard Blanco (2023) and ask students to name what they'd like to discuss. The following are some options:

- **Poems:** Comparing "My Father in English" with "Translation for Mamá"
- **Language:** What more do we learn about Blanco's family and their journey with English?
- **Life Application:** Blanco ends the poem with gratitude for his dad "surrendering the past tense" of his life, which allowed Blanco to "conjugate" himself "in the present of this country." Discuss what that means for Blanco and what that means for us readers. How would we describe any sense of gratitude for what others have done in the past to make something possible in the present?

Lesson #3: Learning a New Language, Learning a New Me: Middle-Grade Fiction

The first (and only) year I was a literacy coach at my K-8 school I had set up this productive color-coded calendar that included planning with teachers, class visits to meet with small groups of students, coteaching, and meetings with administration. This schedule was short-lived, as early on in the school year we had high enrollment in our seventh grade and teachers were needed to teach a new section that was created to make sure we didn't exceed the legal classroom size limit (a parent brought this to the PTA). I stepped into the role of teaching seventh-grade English Language Arts with the lower-elementary literacy coach, teacher Maria Román. We loved transitioning into this role because we knew the students from when they were in our own classrooms and loved planning together. Although we weren't prepared for teaching without having our own classroom space (we traveled to different rooms that were available every day with our books and charts on a cart), we did have support from the administration to design the curriculum to fit the needs of our Spanish, Arabic, and English language speakers.

One of the moments that stood out for me during that school year was when two Arabic-English bilingual students came up to us to discuss their ideas for the informational writing unit. We had started the unit with a focus on text features, immersing students in reading informational texts as they prepared writing pieces on a topic that they had expertise in to teach the rest of the class. The second part of the unit would give them the opportunity to take a different topic to conduct research and focus on how to teach about a subject, citing different sources. These two students expressed concern about how most of the school community would look at them with apprehension, not understanding why they wore their hijabs, whispering behind their backs, and not welcoming them. We listened and encouraged the students to take on the topic they proposed, "Daily Life of a Muslim Teen." What was also clear to us was the doors that would open on addressing cultural misperceptions when you could no longer use language as an excuse for a barrier. In other words, what more could we learn if we moved away from "I don't know their language" to "how can I learn more to understand them" no matter what language the information is in? We could provide translations, glossaries, images, multilingual word charts, and middle-grade literature on the topic as well. I remember that, when I taught sixth grade, we relied a lot on our social studies cluster teacher to recommend multimodal texts to grow our understanding of the lives of young people from different faith backgrounds all over the world (as was part of our curriculum). It is helpful to provide examples of texts that show us how others perceive language-minoritized speakers and what they miss (the rich cultural expressions and connections with another human being) when they make assumptions or disregard them. Marie Arnold's *The Year I Flew Away* addresses these themes from a middle-grade perspective, and I am grateful to have more Haitian voices when we talk about Latine teens.

WRITING LESSON #3

LESSON TEXTS

- *The Year I Flew Away* by Marie Arnold (2021)
- *We Need Diverse Books* blog "Marie Arnold Writes So Immigrant Readers Feel Seen" by Karis Rogerson (2021)

OBJECTIVES

Discussion: Discuss the moments of doubt that can arise for students learning English and the roots of that doubt.

Text Analysis: Apply different reading lenses when revisiting text excerpts to elaborate on ideas.

Writing: Demonstrate how to use different genres (realistic fiction, historical fiction, speculative fiction) to develop a scene focused on a protagonist and how they approach their life challenges.

OPENING DISCUSSION

Invite students to share what they know about learning another language. What worked well for them? What was challenging? Introduce Marie Arnold's book with a brief book blurb and the following quote:

> I wish I could just wake up and suddenly know how to speak English really well. But everyone, including my parents, tells me that it will take time. That doesn't seem fair. The weekend is almost over, and so far all I know how to really say is "Hello, my name is Gabrielle. How are you doing? I am good." Is that enough to help me make friends? (p. 38)

Ask students to share what they think about the advice Gabrielle received. Do they agree? Why or why not? What advice would they give to a newcomer student who is learning English in a new setting and away from their immediate family? This opening discussion aims to facilitate a dialogue on how language learning is integrated with other parts of our being and identity.

TEXT ANALYSIS

When we meet Gabrielle early on in her journey, she has just left Haiti, moved in with her uncle's family in Brooklyn, New York, and started school where the instruction is all in English, not her Haitian Creole. Ask students to read the following excerpts and then reread them with a focus:

- Author's Craft: How does the author use dialogue to move a scene along?
- Author's Craft: How does the author reveal Gabrielle's emotions?
- Character Interpretation: What role does the school librarian, Mrs. Bartell, play in Gabrielle's life? How would you describe her approach in these excerpts?
- Theme Analysis: How do these scenes help us elaborate on the topics of "immigration" and "language learning"? In other words, how do these scenes expand our thinking on immigration from a child's perspective and attending a school where they speak and teach in a language other than your own?

Excerpt #1 from Chapter 3:

> "I'm Mrs. Bartell. I'm the librarian here."
>
> "I am Gabrielle," I reply.
>
> "Your file says you are from Haiti. Is that true?" I nod but don't speak. She smiles at me and says, I am from Haiti too." And then she begins to speak in Haitian Creole to me. I'm relieved. She tells me that there are a lot of families in Brooklyn that came from the Caribbean. There are kids whose families are from Jamaica, Trinidad, and the Dominican Republic.
>
> "They don't talk to me," I say. "I said the wrong thing, and now they hate me."
>
> "No, they don't. Give them a chance to get to know you. You'll make friends; just keep trying. And if you need anything, you can come see me. I'll be in the library. It's on the third floor," she says as she walks me to my class. I stand there in the long hallway looking into the class of kids who already don't like me. (p. 43)

Excerpt #2 from Chapter 3:

> "I read your file, Gabrielle. I know the part of Haiti you come from. I have family there too. It's a hard life, and yet you managed to survive. If you can do that, then you can do anything."
>
> "But I had my mom and dad then. And my friends."

> "Well, now you have me. And I am telling you—you'll be just fine. In fact, you will do really well here. Just remember, you are just as special and just as amazing as the other kids. And don't let anyone tell you differently." (pp. 44–45)

Excerpt #3 from Chapter 3:

> The rest of the day isn't any easier. I have to go to ESL. That means "English as a second language." It's a special class for kids who just came to America and need extra help in English. English is much harder than you think. I can't believe that there are three words that sound exactly the same but mean totally different things. These are the words: *merry, marry,* and *Mary*. Yup, I don't get it.
>
> And then my ESL teacher asks me to say the word *bathroom*, and I do—I say *bafroom*. She says that's not the right way to say it. It's not my fault that the *th* sound is so hard to make. And when school is over, I have to get on that stupid bus again, and again, no one wants to sit with me. (p. 47)

WRITING

Write your own scene for a newcomer in an English class with a small group. Students will have the following options:

- Realistic Fiction: Develop a scene where the newcomer student meets another student who speaks their same home language, and they help each other navigate their ESL class.
- Realistic Fiction: Develop a scene where the newcomer student finds out about an exciting opportunity they are interested in and gets support from their ESL class for the event/audition (acting? athletics? math? science?).
- Historical Fiction (for fans of journalism, current events, and history): Develop a scene where the newcomer student arrives in a new country during a critical time period when epic changes are happening. How are the events in society impacting the newcomer student? How do they respond?
- Speculative Fiction: What if the newcomer student has a special power or a gift (similar to Arnold's character in *The Year I Flew Away*)? What would it be? Would they use it to help them transition into a new country and with a new language? How?

CLOSING DISCUSSION

In the *We Need Diverse Books* blog, "Marie Arnold Writes So Immigrant Readers Feel Seen," (Rogerson, 2021), Haitian author Marie Arnold encourages writers: "Write your personal experiences and not so much to market, because it's very easy to say for example, 'Oh, they're writing about middle-grade werewolves, that's what I'll do!' " she said. "That's fine, but it helps to infuse it with your own personal experiences, especially if you weren't born here if you have outside-of-US experiences. It makes the landscape different; it makes the story different. Don't take yourself out of it, bring in your influences."

Invite small groups to discuss this excerpt or other responses to the questions in the interview and discuss their reactions. What do they believe is the purpose of writing? Another way students can think about this further with excerpts from another author's interview and book is by checking out the short videos on Rebecca Balcárcel's *SixMinuteScholar* YouTube channel (Balcárcel, n.d.), specifically the playlist for her book, *The Other Half of Happy* (2019). Students can consider how Marie Arnold and Rebecca Balcárcel's protagonists navigate their emergent bilingualism and biculturalism in their lives.

Lesson #4: Learning a New Language, Learning a New Me: Anthology

If you are not indigenous to a land, when was the first time you learned about Indigenous peoples and languages? How were they taught if you learned about them in school? Were they only talked about in the past tense? Was it through a land acknowledgement? Did this land acknowledgement also include ways to do right by those Indigenous communities? I ask these questions as a Chilena who didn't learn about the Mapuche Indigenous peoples in Chile until much later in life (through visits to Chile as a teen). I don't recall learning about living Indigenous peoples in the United States in my elementary school, as they were often presented in the past through harmful, erroneous narratives about Thanksgiving. Another major gap in our learning has been the assumption that, if you come from Latin America, you must all speak Spanish! This anti-Indigenous and anti-Black narrative erases the hundreds of Indigenous languages, Haitian Creole, Portuguese, and other languages represented across nations.

At a New York City Public Schools Project Based Learning (PBL) showcase with bi/multilingual students in spring 2024, keynote speaker Dr. Tatyana

Kleyn from City College, City University of New York, asked students what languages were represented in the room. We heard Spanish, Bangla (or Bengali), Arabic, and Quechua. Dr. Kleyn expanded on the importance of including Indigenous languages in our advocacy for language-minoritized students and our school's programming to support students learning English. I loved seeing the Quechua middle grader speak up and represent, not only because I saw the pride in their families' faces but also because all of us in the room could use that reminder. Author Sandra Guzmán's *Daughters of Latin America: An International Anthology of Writing by Latine Women* (2023) includes many of these twenty-four Indigenous languages in this transformative book. Although this book is for adults, I include it in the following lesson as I find excerpts of it useful for our teaching with Latine teens, especially as a representation of what we can do with language(s) and all of the unlearning that needs to happen around minoritized languages.

WRITING LESSON #4

LESSON TEXT

"Karla Sánchez and Yásnaya Elena Aguilar Gil" from *Daughters of Latin America: An International Anthology of Writing by Latine Women* edited by Sandra Guzmán (2023)

OBJECTIVES

Discussion: Discuss the linguistic variety in Mexico.

Text Analysis: Identify cause and effect by observing the connection between colonialism and linguicide (past and present).

Writing: Develop interview questions for writing partnerships to review and share information on Indigenous languages in Mexico.

OPENING DISCUSSION

Editor Sandra Guzmán introduces the conversation between Karla Sánchez and Yásnaya Elena Aguilar Gil with the following:

> In Mexico, in addition to Spanish, more than 365 languages and dialects, grouped in 65 linguistic systems, are spoken. This means that for one year, a different language

> can be spoken every day. That is how linguistically diverse Mexico is. However, most of the population is monolingual and unable to name the Indigenous languages spoken in the region. (p. 75)

What do we know about the languages spoken in Mexico? What can we learn from El Instituto Nacional de Lenguas Indígenas from the government of Mexico?

TEXT ANALYSIS

In this conversation, Yásnaya Elena Aguilar Gil discusses key information on the linguistic diversity in Mexico, how it has changed across the years, and the role that the government ("State") has in making sure Indigenous languages do not disappear. Students can use the following lenses to analyze the four text excerpts below (in small groups or partnerships):

1. Keywords or concepts: Indigenous, language, identity, intervention, linguistic diversity
   a. Identify a term. What does that term mean?
   b. How did we learn about that term?
   c. What examples do we associate with that term?
2. Themes: colonialism, linguicide, myth of mestizaje
   a. What is the connection between these three themes?
   b. What is colonialism's impact on Indigenous languages?
   c. How has the myth of mestizaje taken shape in Mexico? Which populations and languages are erased with the myth of mestizaje?
3. Interview questions
   a. What did the interviewer, Karla Sánchez, ask?
   b. How did the questions allow Yásnaya Elena Aguilar Gil to address the themes above?
   c. What do these questions teach us about interviews or conversations?

Text Excerpt #1:

> According to historians, in 1820, between 65 and 70 percent of the population spoke an Indigenous language [in Mexico] ... In two hundred years, the majority of the Indigenous population was misidentified so now only 6.6 percent of us speak an Indigenous language, and only 11 percent of us identify ourselves as Indigenous. (p. 76)

Text Excerpt #2:

> Erasing mother tongues has been fundamental to the Mexican national project and the creation of the Mexican identity. (p. 77)

Text Excerpt #3:

> Speaking different languages has many advantages at a cognitive and cultural level. But in the case of Mexico, a multilingual society became monolingual because of State intervention. While most of the Indigenous population is bilingual, most of the Spanish-speaking populations is, unfortunately, monolingual. (p. 79)

Text Excerpt #4:

> So, the first thing to do is educate yourself, because you cannot appreciate what you do not know or do not even know exists. We must be aware of linguistic diversity and find enjoyment in it, that you can memorize a song in Nahuatl, learn to read in Maya, and could speak Purépecha. Undoubtedly, learning an Indigenous language is very desirable but also joining the causes of Indigenous nations because there is discrimination and linguistic violence. As a Spanish-speaking person, you can also demand from the State that you have the right to enjoy that linguistic diversity and that it should give you those spaces. (p. 83)

See Appendix C for an Amplifying Counter-narratives graphic (España & Herrera, 2020) to help support students' learning and teaching of these concepts and themes using these text excerpts from *Daughters of Latin America: An International Anthology of Writing by Latine Women.*

WRITING

Ask students to develop interview questions for writing partnerships on the topic of the Indigenous languages in Mexico. Invite students to consider what questions they'd ask each other to teach information on the Indigenous languages in Mexico. They can record this (audio only or audio and video) conversation and save it on a shared classroom digital library to learn from their classmates. First, have students use the following sentence frames to review what they learned:

- "At first, I thought that people from Mexico only spoke ______. After reading this conversation I learned that ..."

- "Before Mexico was colonized, Indigenous languages made up ______ percent of ______. Now, speakers of Indigenous languages only make up ______ percent of ______."
- "A multilingual society in Mexico became a monolingual society due to ..."
- "Linguistic diversity means ..."
- "It is important that Mexico's government ______ because ..."

Next, students can create questions based on that information. For example:

- What new information did you learn?
- What is the impact of colonization on Indigenous languages?
- What does linguistic diversity mean?
- What can the Mexican government do to help speakers of Indigenous languages?

CLOSING DISCUSSION

Editor Sandra Guzmán introduces the *Daughters of Latin America: An International Anthology of Writing by Latine Women* anthology by asking "what happens when a language is lost?" and stating that "languages are like flora and fauna—they define a people, a nation, a culture, a cosmology" (p. 7). Encourage students to consider ways their classroom and schoolwide communities can welcome and learn about the linguistic diversity of their classmates' homelands or the places they learned about in this lesson sequence. What will they do differently with this knowledge? How will this new knowledge contribute to a stronger sense of solidarity with and for those not just learning English but also developing other languages and cultures?

TESTIMONIO: Coral Zayas

Administrator for New York City Public Schools; Adjunct Lecturer, Brooklyn College, City University of New York

One of my lifelong mentors and former Hunter College professor from my graduate studies in bilingual education, Dr. Yvonne de Gaetano, introduced me to Coral. I've known her for over a decade, and I've seen Coral go from classroom teaching to coaching and now supporting all of New York City Public Schools!

CORAL ON HER JOURNEY AS AN EDUCATOR:

When I first started teaching, I was teaching sixth-grade transitional bilingual English and Spanish in Inwood, New York. At that point, I taught all the content areas. So I taught reading, writing, math, science, and social studies. Then I taught social studies through ENL [English as a New Language] methodology. So that was fully in English for every student with a lot of project-based learning, group work, trips, and museums. We kind of lived at the Met [Metropolitan Museum of Art].

I became a Math and Science Dual Language teacher for the next eight years. I was also teaching Bilingual Literacy at Hunter College. That kind of kept me with one foot in the math and sciences but also one foot in literacy.

And then an opportunity opened up at a K to 8 school … An amazing growth journey. To become a literacy coach … After a few years, I asked to come back to the classroom … It was during COVID … We needed more teachers in the classrooms.

Then I had an opportunity to collaborate in a different school, that was an elementary school, as a coach but with a principal who I was much more aligned [with] in pedagogical philosophy practices and just leadership styles … When I became a Multilingual and English Language Learner Services Administrator, I started visiting schools all over District 30, building relationships with principals, teachers, even students. I was involved in district-level decision-making, and it really gave me a sense of the widespread influence that these people in these positions have … We are encouraging teachers to bring artifacts that require students to use their languages … It's really powerful to be in this [position], guiding them in creating these translanguaging spaces, bilingual spaces within these blue and red zones, and now having what I'm calling a "purple zone" that is visible and celebrated, that we don't hide it.

CORAL ON HER FIRST MEMORY OF SEEING HERSELF AS A WRITER:

The feeling of awkwardness and being unprepared is the first thing that comes up. I was never taught to be a writer in my schooling in Puerto Rico. We didn't write stories and we didn't write poetry. We learned to read it and wrote about it. But we were not authors so that concept when I became a teacher here of "we are all authors" and having a writer's notebook, it was so uncomfortable to me. And yet I learned to be a writing teacher. I saw myself as a coach.

CORAL ON HER FAVORITE WRITING ACTIVITY WITH LATINX TEENS:

Most of my teaching career was in mathematics. Because I was a biliteracy adjunct at Hunter College, I knew how important it was for students to develop biliteracy. My favorite assignment was a mathematical autobiography. Each paragraph was dedicated to a different mathematical skill: counting, adding/subtracting, multiplying/dividing, and fractions. There can be a lot of trauma around math instruction which is why I wanted it to be understandable for my students. With this autobiography, I encouraged them to use their language.

CORAL ON LATINX AUTHORS GIVING HER LIFE RIGHT NOW:

Elizabeth Acevedo came up for me. I use her poetry with children and adults in master's level programs. I think her writing is so beautiful, so poignant, so relevant to a lot of our youth and their families, and us as women, grown adults right now. I will read anything she writes.

CORAL'S ADVICE FOR WRITING TEACHERS OF LATINX YOUTH:

Just let them write! ... A lot of our students are stuck when they're being asked to write ... You can turn that into anything through the writing process.

CORAL ON WRITING SHE'S WORKING ON NOW:

I am writing guidance documents citywide. I wrote a lot of the bilingual program descriptions. Now, I'm collaborating on one about biliteracy.

Chapter Five

Vamos a resolver y florecer: Resourcefulness, Resilience, and Recovery

"Las ganas de echar adelante y de obtener un título universitario y tener un buen trabajo porque aquí no se puede vivir con el sueldo mínimo y para eso hay que trabajar duro."

—Paola, undergraduate, Childhood Education with a Bilingual Extension

I teach at a public commuter college where 23 percent of the undergraduate student body is made up of Latinx students, 22 percent are Black or African American, and 24 percent are Asian (Brooklyn College City University of New York Office of the Associate Provost for Institutional Effectiveness, n.d.). Most students hold a job while completing a full courseload of five courses a semester (especially the education majors with concentrations in Puerto Rican and Latinx Studies or those with a minor in Childhood and Youth Studies, Psychology, or other common studies paired with education). Several of them are also the first in their family to attend college. Paola came from the Dominican Republic as an adult with her partner and children, and she dreams of completing her college education. She transferred from a community college where she completed her associate degree and joined our college to obtain her bachelor's. I asked Paola what helped her confront the challenges in her life when she moved from the Dominican Republic to New York City. Like several other undergraduate students and future teachers, she recalled the "ganas de echar adelante," or the will to progress in life. For Paola, this included the goals of obtaining a college degree and a good job that would pay more than the minimum wage, because that is not sustainable. Paola went on to describe the sacrifice and efforts required to meet her goals. The semester following this interview, Paola began the Bilingual Pupil Services internship at New York City Public Schools while caring for her two children and remaining a full-time undergraduate student. Although Paola doesn't lack ganas, this took a toll on her overall wellness as she tried her best to remain above water with her courses, lesson planning, parenting, and partnership.

I spent a year teaching middle-grade English at an independent private school in Westchester, New York, and I'll never forget the "ponte las pilas" framed sign that an elementary teacher gifted me at the end of the school year. It was a tough year for both of us. We were the few Latinas on faculty, and we struggled not just with a sense of belonging but also with a sense of feeling as if our talents could be used to the maximum in an environment that felt like some could not see the fullness of who we were and our potential. I displayed the "ponte las pilas" sign in my office for the remaining weeks, a reminder to keep pushing to achieve my goals in the next stage in my life. Although "ponte las pilas" directly translates to "put on your batteries," this idiomatic expression can be a motivation for some, especially as a reminder of this phrase that was told to them throughout their adolescence. For others, it can be somewhat triggering as it pushes forth the dominant narrative of working yourself to an almost breaking point. Especially for working-class Latinx immigrants, children of immigrants, first-generation students, and eldest siblings, the tide may be changing from "ponte las pilas" to “caring for myself is not self-indulgence, it is self-preservation, and that is an act of political warfare,” as Audre Lorde reminded us (1988). I’m part of this latter group. This is where this chapter stands: living in the tension between resilience —often asked of Latinx youth amid layers of institutional barriers—and recovery. How do we honor the sacrifices made by those who paved the way for us while listening to our drive and our bodies in our paths to achieving our goals? How can we use our voices to highlight the challenges and realities of enacting our resourcefulness while advocating for our much-deserved thriving and rest?

My poem “‘Ponte las pilas’ ... is Canceled,” inspired by Dilruba Ahmed’s “Phase One” and Pádraig Ó Tuama’s essay on Ahmed’s breathtaking work, is my way of meditating on those questions from the perspective of my high school self. By that point, I was very much aware of the sacrifices my parents made to bring me to the United States and the sacrifices they continued making as I watched my dad work in maintenance and my mom clean houses. I took advantage of all of the opportunities offered to me in high school: Advanced Placement courses, college credit courses (thank you, Borough of Manhattan Community College and Pace University partnerships), National Honor Society, Financial Women’s Association mentoring program, Distributive Education Clubs of America (business club), Estée Lauder internship, Christian Club, and Student Government. To be honest, I was exhausted just thinking back to all of my extracurricular activities as I wrote this introduction and poem! I knew my church involvement and high grades wouldn’t be enough to compete with those students from more privileged backgrounds who’d submit impressive college applications. I also couldn’t compete with college applicants whose parents attended college. I wasn’t a legacy student or one who could afford the tuition at private colleges. So, I “put on my batteries” and did the best I could. My “‘Ponte las Pilas’ ... is Canceled” poem is what I wish high school Carla would’ve heard back then and what I hope to share with my child when she is older.

Poem: “ ‘Ponte las pilas’ ... is Canceled”

For joining Student Government
where planning skills were birthed,
while working your first job,
pushing the skills to network,
I forgive you.

For feeling (church girl) guilt and joy while performing
your Titanic theme song routine,
while staying after school for math tutoring,
focusing on making parents proud by making the National Honor Society,
I forgive you.

For saving face in the College and Careers Magazine interview,
smiles you had to keep,
burying financial aid concerns and screams,
pushing forth in DECA competitions on small business studies,
while papá would repeatedly dash those familia España empanada spot dreams
(learned about what it meant to have capital to invest real quickly),
I forgive you.

For representing Chile with folklore attire on Multicultural Day celebration,
finally on the map for conversations in school about la tierra que me vio nacer,
trying to make up for all the years away from family,
while immigration laws keep nostalgia at bay,
I forgive you. I forgive
you.

We are canceling "ponte las pilas."
In its place, we will whisper
"Descansa,"
pass you a blanket and a pillow,
and you'll nap.

We will ask, "How can we help?"
Checking in on one another,
and take collective deep breaths.

Realistic Fiction Narrative: "Self-Portrait with Cropped Hair"

Host and producer of *La Brega: Stories of the Puerto Rican Experience* Alana Casanova-Burgess said the following when asked about the tropes that are common around Puerto Rico:

> In the first English episode of La Brega, I have this montage on the word resilience. It's on how mainstream outlets in the United States talk about the challenges in Puerto Rico—these poor people who are so good at being resilient and congratulating Puerto Ricans on being so tough. That came up in coverage of New Orleans after Hurricane Katrina as well, the idea that if you have a group of people who are struggling and trying to recover from a natural disaster and then, even though the state does not respond adequately to their needs, we sort of celebrate that resilience, instead of questioning why resilience is needed in first place.
>
> (González Martínez, 2021BIB_000_0053)

I, too, have heard these narratives of resilience about the Puerto Rican community, not only as a faculty member in an Ethnic Studies department but also as a literacy partner for a second-grade team at a bilingual school in El Barrio, New York, that had students from Puerto Rico enrolled after Hurricane Maria. The narrative is often one that is in awe of a community that comes together to rebuild and renew, but it is rare to hear critiques of institutions and governments about the root causes of that resilience. In other words, why would the lives of children who have lost family members and the roof over their heads, and who need to move to start life anew, need to be uprooted in the first place?

I've been thinking a lot about the resilience that is lauded and asked of children, especially after the COVID-19 pandemic shutdown of 2020, as well as the months of online and hybrid learning. The summer before most of us went into shutdown, I had moved away from a neighborhood in Queens, New York, to a suburb north of the city. A few months after my move, that same neighborhood was a pandemic epicenter. I remember while we were teaching online, there were conversations about the lessons we were learning, how much we'd prioritize social-emotional learning (SEL), how much more support we needed for mental health, and how young people would need all kinds of mentorship to make it through the next stages in their lives. Yet, I write this book during the time of book bans; the elimination of SEL, and Diversity, Equity, and Inclusion in several states; and violent arrests of students protesting on college campuses. So I ask, what did we learn, and which groups of students are most impacted? This is happening while young people navigate the day-to-day. In "Self-Portrait with Cropped Hair," a fictional narrative excerpt from a larger work inspired by my life, I give readers a glimpse into two characters I've been developing as a way to help me process the resourcefulness, resilience, and recovery that's asked of Latinx youth while they grapple with systemic injustices and seldom have a moment to exist.

"Did you reach out to me because you need money?" Gretchen asks as we stand in front of Frida Kahlo's *Self-Portrait with Cropped Hair*. She looks through her purse, and I just stare ahead at Frida. We were on our monthly trip with our mentoring program, this time at the Museum of Modern Art. I can't bear to look at my girls around me and avoid Gretchen's gaze. You'd think a mentor would be more perceptive. Why would she think I reached out to her for money? I sent her an email last week, trying my best to make my "Communication Studies" teacher at my business high school proud of my "formal" writing skills:

Dear Gretchen,
Thank you for your recommendation. I sent the job application, and they told me they would let me know in two weeks. I would also like to speak with you about something on our next trip. It's really important. I hope we can talk after the museum visit. Do you have some time?
Thank you,
Alejandra

Gretchen sees me three times a week at her office for my part-time job besides our monthly trips. She's a financial planner. I'm an "international business" major at my high school, so they matched us for the program and for potential paid internships. I file her clients' files, type out her expenses, and answer her phones. I rush to her office on Fifth Avenue Mondays through Wednesdays after school for three hours. It makes my parents proud, and they swear it'll make me super smart with my money. I even get paid five dollars more than minimum wage, and all my friends say how lucky I am. I feel good helping my parents out when I get that paycheck, but sometimes, working with her and at that office makes me uncomfortable. I get that same sick feeling in my gut that I have right now.

I ignore her comment and hope no one heard her, but it's a museum, and though you'd think people would whisper, she doesn't. I look at the other girls from school and see they're trying their best to pretend they didn't hear. They walk as a group to the next painting. I see Dana and just want to cry.

"Alejandra, have you seen this one over here?" she yells in my direction.

She's another one that doesn't whisper. Ever. Dana always knows when I need saving.

"Girl, I just want to tell her I was thinking about putting a music minor on my college applications. I don't know if that will look bad or if it's a waste, you know? That's all. She's in it. She has her job, her fancy office, and her fancy apartment. I want that, too. It's the least I could do to help my parents out, you know? Could I study both business and music?"

"I don't know Alejandra. I know you're good and all with our math and business classes but you look so bored! I can't stand looking at your cara larga! I don't know how these teachers even look at your stank face in class!"

I laugh so hard (at myself?) my stomach hurts. She's so right.

"I've heard you sing, I've read your songs, and you're really good. You're so happy in our poetry group, too! It's like Fridays after school you're a different person for spoken word. Why are you even going for a business major?"

I know I should answer this, but Dana won't take my well-rehearsed college application answer. She's been my number-one fan. At every school performance, every spoken-word poetry contest, even at the shows I've put on for family, she's clapping or snapping away.

"Well, are you applying to colleges away from home?" was my non-response. I knew this was a touchy subject for her but I didn't feel like answering her question.

"You know I can't leave New York. It's different for me. I can't just leave mami." Dana takes her hand off of my back and moves away. I know this hurts her, but it hurts me too.

How is it that Dana is so badass at school but at home she barely speaks her mind? Maybe it's because she has two younger brothers who adore her and her mom is all they have. No other family, well besides my family. We've spent every holiday together since middle school! I call her mom tía because we're that close. Tía Yuleiky's family disowned her and her kids once she left her husband. I don't call him tío. We refer to him as el pastelito or el pastel. I heard my mom call him that once and it just stuck. You'd think a cake would be a good thing but in this case when I overheard my mom and tía talking about "ese pastel se la cree muy hombre gritándote," I knew it was a bad thing. I could never call him my uncle knowing he was screaming at tía.

This happened the first week of high school and no one has been the same since. Tía Yuleiky said "no más pendejo" after he threw a lamp at her. She had decided to go back to school and get her associate's degree and he was not having it. He demanded she stay home. She demanded he let her be happy. Tía thought things would change when she compromised and took some classes online but it made things worse. "Tienes que tener paciencia, es que los hombres son así," her own mother told her. Her own mother told her to be patient because that's just the way men are! Everyone in her family told her it was her fault and that she should just let him be the man of the house. Tía Yuleiky wasn't about to let him control her and treat her that way.

Maybe if Dana just told her mom how she felt then she'd understand. I know she doesn't want to leave her mom alone with her brothers but wouldn't her mom want her to be happy just like she wanted that happiness for herself?

I whisper, "I'm sorry" and hold Dana's hand. This friendship is too precious and with these big life decisions we need each other.

I see Gretchen coming. "Gretchen, I sent you that message because I need some college advice. Not money." I take a deep breath.

"Well, I thought you needed money because of your college applications but college advice? You should really ask your college counselor. I went to college a really long time ago and both my children went to my husband's alma mater after they explored their interests," Gretchen says as she places a hand on my shoulder.

"You're right. I'll ask my college counselor," I nod and look for the group as I shift my body, letting her hand fall off my shoulder. It's best to keep it short and simple. These museum trips are long, and I really don't want to keep talking. We're already way behind our tour guide and the group.

"I just don't want to steer you in the wrong direction," Gretchen says, and I can tell she feels bad.

We walk towards the group, and I take another look at the Frida painting. "Mira que si te quise, fué por el pelo, ahora que estás pelona, ya no te quiero" it says and I feel like she's looking at me. Like she's trying to tell me something. Seeing her chopped hair and that defiant look. I can almost hear her say "soy yo y qué, ¿qué vas a hacer o decirme?" as if telling me "This is me and what? What are you going to tell me or do about it?" Maybe she's passing the scissors along to me. Like I'm next. It's my move. Will I ever have her courage?

"Alexandra, we're leaving to the fourth floor," Gretchen calls me to go.

I take a deep breath, take one final look at Frida, ask for her blessing, and say, "It's Alejandra. I'm ready."

National Honor Society Award ceremony at Murry Bergtraum High School in New York City

TEACHER TEXT SET

1. Media (podcasts):
   a. *La Brega*
   b. *Radio Ambulante*
   c. *In the Thick*
   d. *Alt.Latino*
2. Articles:
   a. National Research Center on Hispanic Children and Family's "Latinx Families' Strengths and Resilience Contribute to Their Well-being"
   b. International Journal of Qualitative Studies in Education, Volume 33, Issue 8: "Understanding Latina/o Resilience" (2020)
   c. "Will the Media Get Past the 'Resiliency' of Puerto Ricans?" by Erica González Martínez for Women's Media Center
   d. "The Burden of Acting Human: Rethinking Race, Class, and Gender Experiences in U.S. Independent Schools" by Angel Rubiel González—video summary of the article with the author on Teachers College Record (2024) Vimeo
3. Books:
   a. *For Brown Girls with Sharp Edges and Tender Hearts: A Love Letter to Women of Color* by Prisca Dorca Mojica Rodríguez
   b. *We Are Not from Here* by Jenny Torres Sanchez
   c. *Manteca! An Anthology of* Afro-Latin@ *Poets* edited by Melissa Castillo-Garsow
   d. *Living Beyond Borders: Growing Up Mexican in Ameria* edited by Margarita Longoria
4. Recommended social media accounts:
   a. @latinxparenting
   b. @hip_latina
   c. @latinarebels

LESSON SEQUENCE OVERVIEW AND STUDENT TEXT SET Vamos a resolver y florecer: Resourcefulness, Resilience, and Recovery			
Lesson #1	**Lesson #2**	**Lesson #3**	**Lesson #4**
America Ferrera's monologue in the *Barbie* film America Ferrera's TED Talk, "My Identity is a Superpower"	"Yesenia Montilla: Poet Profile" by Jasminne Mendez "a brief meditation on breath" by Yesenia Montilla	*Frizzy* by Claribel A. Ortega, illustrated by Rose Bousamra	"American Street: The American Dream and the Immigrant Imagination," Ibi Zoboi presentation at Vanderbilt University *American Street* by Ibi Zoboi

Lesson #1: Vamos a resolver y florecer: Resourcefulness, Resilience, and Recovery: A Multimodal Introduction

I always know I can get a good laugh with social media posts that make fun of the typical lines immigrant kids hear growing up about the challenges the older generation had attending school. You know the ones I'm talking about! They start with "when I was your age" and might continue with something like "I would walk miles and miles to school." I can't help but let out a chuckle when the person in the video acts out those conversations, with chanclas and heavy bags, emphasizing the difficulty of that trip to school or showing images of dilapidated buildings, books, and buses. All of these were associated with their childhood.

I've been following America Ferrera's career for quite some time now, impressed by how she navigates different spaces that include people like her, and those who have no idea where she and her family are coming from. I return to her TED Talk, "My Identity is a Superpower" (TED, 2019), often as I consider the "when I was your age" talks from my family and the expectations from those outside of our family circles. I'm most concerned about the stereotypes and limitations that our Latine students face. Interviews with America Ferrera and her TED Talk are great texts to facilitate a discussion on this reality.

WRITING LESSON #1

LESSON TEXTS

- America Ferrera's monologue in the *Barbie* film (Max, 2023)
- America Ferrera's TED Talk, "My Identity is a Superpower" (TED, 2019)

OBJECTIVES

Discussion: Discuss the expectations others place on us and those we place on ourselves.

Text Analysis: Understand how the structure of a TED Talk supports the development of an idea with memorable moments.

Writing: Develop an annotated outline for a TED Talk to share ideas on expectations, perceptions, and their impact on our lives.

OPENING DISCUSSION

Invite students to think about the expectations others place on them and those they place on themselves by first watching or reading America Ferrera's monologue in the *Barbie* film (Max, 2023). Students can take on some of the topics addressed in the monologue in a small group, with each group noticing the structure of the speech:

"You have to be … but not too …"
"You have to be … but also …"

Students can consider the expectations for women from the monologue:

- Body size
- Wealth
- Leadership
- Career
- Beauty

In closing the monologue, America Ferrera says, "I'm just so tired of watching myself and every single woman tie herself into knots so that people will like us" (Max, 2023). Ask students to consider how the expectations might be different for different women, men, and gender-expansive people (by race, sexuality, immigration status, ethnicity, etc.). How do these expectations compare to the expectations people have of you?

TEXT ANALYSIS

Use the following excerpts and guiding questions to understand how America Ferrera structured and shared her ideas in a TED Talk:

1. "I kept receiving the same message again and again and again. That my identity was an obstacle I had to overcome. And so I thought, 'Come at me, obstacle. I'm an American. My name is America. I trained my whole life for this, I'll just follow the playbook, I'll work harder.' " [4:05–4:31]

   Identify the messages that America Ferrera was internalizing. How do they compare to those delivered in the *Barbie* film monologue? What do those expectations in her life reveal about how people in the entertainment industry viewed her?

2. Compare America Ferrera working her "hardest to overcome all the things people said were wrong" with the ways you have faced expectations that others have had of you that didn't match what you wanted for yourself. For example, for America, this meant she would straighten her hair, try to stay out of the sun to not get "too brown," and dress differently. [4:32–5:02]
3. "In spite of what I had been told my whole life, I saw firsthand that people actually did want to see stories about people like me. And that my unrealistic expectations to see myself authentically represented in the culture were other people's expectations, too." [6:02–6:19]

   Describe the changes that America Ferrera witnessed. How did these changes reveal the types of stories people wanted to see? How did these changes impact America?

4. "Just a few years ago, my agent called to explain to me why I wasn't getting a role in a movie. He said, 'They loved you and they really, really do want to cast diversely, but the movie isn't financeable until they cast the white role first.' He delivered the message with a broken heart and with a tone that communicated, 'I understand how messed up this is.' But nonetheless, just like hundreds of times

before, I felt the tears roll down my face. And the pang of rejection rise up in me and then the voice of shame scolding me, 'You are a grown woman, stop crying over a job.' I went through this process for years of accepting the failure as my own and then feeling deep shame that I couldn't overcome the obstacles. But this time, I heard a new voice. A voice that said, 'I'm tired. I've had enough.' A voice that understood my tears and my pain were not about losing a job. They were about what was actually being said about me." [9:39–10:52]

Analyze the tension in this reality that America faced when feeling shame and exhaustion while pushing forth to be accepted. What caused the exhaustion and the shame? Why would others' perceptions about America impact her this way?

WRITING

By this point in their lives, students have experienced their share of expectations placed on them. Some expectations have resulted in students pushing forward and trying to meet those expectations, while others have resulted in them pushing back and challenging those expectations.

Option #1: Have students revisit the TED Talk to understand the structure of the piece. They can annotate the transcript of America's TED Talk by noting the following: How does it begin? How does America build up to "I'm tired. I've had enough."? How does America end? What do each of these points teach us when we are sharing memorable moments from our lives? Compare your notes with the "TEDx Speaker Guide" outline, which you can locate by searching TEDx Speaker Guide online.

Option #2: Ask students to create an annotated outline of America Ferrera's TED Talk.

Option #3: If doing this across a few days, you can build up to students creating an annotated outline for their own TED Talk on expectations, perceptions, and their impact on our lives. Students can consider what they'd borrow from America Ferrera's TED Talk, what they'd do differently, and what they'd feel comfortable sharing with their class.

CLOSING DISCUSSION

Invite students to share one line from their annotated TED Talk outlines. The line can be from America Ferrera's TED Talk or the one they created for themselves. After each student shares a line out loud (or on an interactive document), the class can discuss their observations:

- How do these lines reflect what we have in common?
- How do these lines reveal differences in our experiences?
- What are our takeaways for considering how we'll navigate conversations on our identities, expectations placed on us, the expectations we place on ourselves, and how we can continue without burning ourselves out?

Lesson #2: Vamos a resolver y florecer: Resourcefulness, Resilience, and Recovery: Poetry

One of my favorite times of the year as a middle-grade teacher was always teaching a poetry unit. Although I'd include poetry throughout the year, there was something special about having a dedicated time across a few weeks to truly immerse ourselves in poets, poetry, and our writing. Maybe it's because I come from the land of Pablo Neruda and Gabriela Mistral, or because of my church-girl teen years songwriting and analyzing religious texts, or maybe it's the fact that I've always loved music and found poetry as a way to witness the world.

But I know that in this list I have to include the students who shook me to my core with their poetry. Luisito, one of my sixth graders, wrote an extended metaphor poem on life being an empty playground with no one to play with. Aileen wrote a poem on her bilingualism that she performed after a Silk Road Ensemble artist performed in our class and she was moved to share her story through this poem (España & Herrera, 2020, p. 138). Whether we laughed, cried, pooled our rage into a sea of rage, poetry units were when I had the most fun playing with words and getting to know my students—even the ones who were jaded by that point and thought our poetry unit would be about checking off checklists of figurative language. Even those reluctant poets turned it around when we approached poetry as a way of living. We took community walks; we returned to our personal and fictional narratives, turning some entries into poems; we watched spoken word and tried some of our own performances. This is the vibe (as the youth say/said) we want all of the time, especially when gasping for air in difficult moments when it seems like the poets and other artists are the ones who are helping us make our way. Yesenia Montilla is that poet for this time. You will find "a brief meditation on breath" a poem that is situated in a specific time/event and yet is timeless. It's the meditation we need to survive in these times.

WRITING LESSON #2

LESSON TEXTS

- "Yesenia Montilla: Poet Profile" by Jasminne Mendez (2018)
- "a brief meditation on breath" by Yesenia Montilla (2020)

OBJECTIVES

Discussion: Discuss our feelings on what it takes to survive in our world.

Text Analysis: Explain a poet's use of imagery and repetition.

Writing: Create a poem that extends a metaphor in response to Yesenia Montilla's "a brief meditation on breath."

OPENING DISCUSSION

Select a few excerpts from Jasminne Mendez's *Poet Profile* blog on Yesenia Montilla (2018) to introduce students to this poet and our topic. You may want to focus on the responses to questions on identity and writing. Wrap up your opening discussion by calling attention to Yesenia Montilla's response to the question about what else she's working on:

> "Surviving. Seriously, this world has me so twisted and it is A JOB to wake up every day and try to live in JOY and in love. So I have dreams, I want to write plays, and short stories and movies, but at this moment survival is pretty much my full time job." (Mendez, 2018)

How do students feel about this response? How does this response help them understand other responses in this interview?

TEXT ANALYSIS

The poem "a brief meditation on breath" (Montilla, 2020) has layers of meaning and references to events. It was written during the COVID-19 pandemic shutdown in 2020. You may want to consider the following ways to help students analyze the text:

1. Read the text once.
2. Return to it in small groups to have students discuss the title and all the references or connections to breath in the poem.
3. Select one literary device (imagery, repetition) to focus on as a class to make the connection between the use of this device and understanding what Yesenia Montilla is saying about breath.
4. End by having students share their reactions to one line that evoked a strong reaction from them.

WRITING

Read the part of Yesenia Montilla's poem "a brief meditation on breath" that includes "i am a ball of tense / living" (Montilla, 2020).

Have students return to their annotated outlines from the previous lessons or any writing that they can revisit on how their bodies, minds, and entire being react to the resilience that is asked of them (or those people they studied/read like America Ferrera and Yesenia Montilla) in the face of obstacles. Students can work on turning that writing into a stanza like this excerpt, which can eventually be a standalone poem or a seed for developing a longer poem on the topic. If necessary, students can borrow the structure from the excerpt:

> "Sometimes I [describe an action related to breathing],
> my [describe how the body shows this],
> I am a ball of [describe how you are living],
> [create a metaphor that connects with that description of living this way]"

CLOSING DISCUSSION

Invite students to discuss Yesenia Montilla's "About this Poem" section on "a brief meditation on breath" on the Academy of American Poets *Poem-a-Day* site (Montilla, 2020). Students can discuss what they learn from this context, the meaning of freedom, and how these words help them think about their lives. You may want to focus on the following excerpt and the connections Yesenia Montilla makes between breathing, the pandemic, and George Floyd.

"I could not help but make the correlation between the inability to take in breath—a symptom of COVID-19 and the loss of breath at the hands of the police—a reality of being Black in America. This was before we knew that this virus would take us in such higher numbers compared to white folks. This was before George Floyd and all that has happened and continues to happen and will continue to happen as we try to get free." (Montilla, 2020)

Lesson #3: Vamos a resolver y florecer: Resourcefulness, Resilience, and Recovery: Middle-Grade Fiction

Teaching Latine teens meant my days were never the same! Even now, as an undergraduate professor of Puerto Rican and Latinx Studies, my students (encompassing a group beyond Latinx teens) keep me on my toes. It's never a dull moment when you teach young people who can school you on life and your teaching! One of my favorite memories was when I brought the *Black in Latin America* documentary with Professor Henry Louis Gates, Jr. (2011) into conversations, along with picture books and middle-grade novels on the topics of Blackness, beauty, and migration. What I had assumed would be seamless discussions using guiding questions from the documentary and book club protocols all erupted in (good) chaos when the views in the classroom differed on the Dominican students' interpretation of their heritage. I did so much more listening than lecturing, trying to understand where my students were coming from with their comments on straight hair vs. curly hair, their ideas on skin color and privilege, and their questions on how to self-identify when they're in their homelands vs. in the United States. Although the *Black in Latin America* documentary gave us the language to describe many of the patterns we were noticing, I knew we needed more accessible texts for this age group and was happy to pause and partner it with picture books and middle-grade novels.

Frizzy (2022) by Claribel A. Ortega is the book I wish had existed back then! Ortega and illustrator Rose Bousamra created an absolutely beautiful graphic novel that tackles so much of what my students were yearning to discuss. Yes, they loved their families, and yes, they wanted to spend time with them, but why were they only complimented or told that they looked good when they got rid of anything natural like their curls or even darker skin color (we had a lot of discussions on famous athletes who promoted skin-whitening products)? *Frizzy*, or *Rizos* in the Spanish translation (2023), is the book we should all read to help us think about the ways we interact with loved ones when we do not necessarily agree or when parts of the conversations always seem to be missing, especially those difficult parts having to do with colonization and proximity to whiteness.

I loved being in conversation with author Claribel A. Ortega and middle-school students on *Frizzy* for the 2023 Latinx KidLit Book Festival event (Latinx KidLit Book Festival, 2023).

WRITING LESSON #3

LESSON TEXT

Frizzy (2022) by Claribel A. Ortega, illustrated by Rose Bousamra

OBJECTIVES

Discussion: Discuss how the illustrations in a graphic novel help us understand the story better.

Text Analysis: Examine perspectives in a text.

Writing: Create a scene that reveals how a character deals with the tension of trying to be themselves and live joyfully while facing different expectations from loved ones.

OPENING DISCUSSION

Show students the illustrations from the first chapter of Claribel A. Ortega's *Frizzy* (2022). Discuss how the illustrations help us get to know the following:

- Setting: The chapter is titled "El Salon," and the illustrations have several details on what the Dominican hair salon looks like and the surrounding neighborhood.
- Characters: Observe the characters' facial expressions. Notice how these give us a sense of how they feel in the hair salon.
- Theme: The book is called *Frizzy* and shows a character with curly hair on the cover. How do the illustrations in this first chapter show us how the different characters feel about curly hair (protagonist, mother, hair stylist)?

TEXT ANALYSIS

Read Chapter 1 in *Frizzy* and return to these excerpts when you finish the chapter:

Marlene: "Why do I have to get my hair done **again**, Mami? We were just here three days ago—**OUCH!**"

(p. 3)

Mom: "And **I'm** tired of having this argument every week. Don't you want to look nice for Diana's quince? The **whole family** will be there Marlene. We have to make a good impression."

(p.6)

Marlene: "**FLOWERS?**"
Mom: "It's so **cute**!"
Marlene: "I look like a **meadow**."
Hair stylist: "No, you look **presentable**."

(pp. 13–14)

Students can begin by identifying the different perspectives in the text about curly hair. What does the mom think about Marlene's natural curls? What does the mom think about how they should all look for Marlene's cousin's quinceañera? What does the hairstylist in this Dominican salon think about the curls? What does Marlene think about her hair and having to spend so much time straightening it in the hair salon?

Students can move into discussing how we know these perspectives from the author's craft (use of dialogue, punctuation, revealing actions) and the illustrations.

WRITING

Share the following prompt with students:

Using Ortega's graphic novel as a mentor text, consider the times in your life when you've had a different perspective on your life than a loved one. Select one of those times to focus on developing that scene in writing. Write down what was said, when it was said, and how you learned more about yourself and others during one of those interactions.

It may help to have a chart listing what you noticed in Ortega's graphic novel and what you'd like to include in your own scene. For example:

Observations on Claribel A. Ortega's *Frizzy*:
What I'd like to try in my scene:
Questions I have about my writing/Support I'll need:

Setting:
Character descriptions (in writing or in the illustrations):
Dialogue:
Actions:
Inner dialogue/thoughts:

CLOSING DISCUSSION

Option #1: Have students share their scenes in writing partnerships or groups. After sharing their scenes, each writing partnership or group can create a list of the topics their scenes addressed. For example, in *Frizzy*, we read about standards of beauty related to hair, specifically how curly hair wasn't accepted by certain family members (in the rest of the book, we meet another family member who embraces their natural curls and teaches Marlene how to care for her hair). Students may have other topics that relate to the topic of how to address expectations, be yourself fully, and recover from the negative messages around them.

Option #2: If you would like to show *Frizzy*'s arc to further discussions on resourcefulness, resilience, and recovery, you may want to show a panel or two from "The Plan" and "A Special Wash Day" chapters. In "The Plan," Marlene's cousin's visit makes matters worse when she is described as having "good hair" while Marlene tries to resolve her hair issues on her own. In "A Special Wash Day," there's a pocket of hope with Marlene's Tía Ruby, who teaches Marlene how to care for her curls and love herself. These chapters may inspire students to consider interactions with characters in their scenes (and people in their lives) who offer support and validating words.

Lesson #4: Vamos a resolver y florecer: Resourcefulness, Resilience, and Recovery: Young Adult Realistic Fiction

When Ibi Zoboi arrived on my school's campus for an author visit, I knew our students and faculty would be blown away. I had been teaching middle-grade English at seventh and eighth grade, had been following Zoboi's work for years at literacy conferences and was thrilled to create this space for students and faculty to be introduced to her work and career. Not only did Ibi Zoboi speak to our students but she tailored her talks to the lower and upper middle grades, sharing about her book *My Life as an Ice Cream Sandwich* (2019) with the fifth and sixth graders, and her other books like *Star Child: A Biographical Constellation of Octavia Estelle Butler* (2022), *Black Enough: Stories of Being Young and Black in America* (2020), and *American Street* (2017), with seventh and eighth graders. She talked about her journey from Haiti and her identity as a writer.

When I organized an event for my college campus on "Young Adult Literature and the Latinx Diaspora" (2023) (see the event archived on the Brooklyn College Ethyle R. Wolfe Institute for the Humanities YouTube channel), I knew my undergraduate students needed to meet her! This time, Ibi Zoboi talked about *Nigeria Jones* (2023), her novel about a protagonist growing up with a Black nationalist father, navigating not only her sense of identity but also sense of community with a Black separatist group and a predominantly white educational institution. This book went on to become a National Book Award Finalist, and it won the Coretta Scott King author award! You'll see in the following lesson, with excerpts from *American Street* (2017) and a lecture on "The American Dream and the Immigrant Imagination" (Vanderbilt University, 2019), that Ibi Zoboi is a beautiful storyteller and a mentor for all of the writers in our classes. I hope you are encouraged in your own writing to take up some of the recurring themes in your life and take inspiration from Ibi Zoboi.

WRITING LESSON #4

LESSON TEXTS

- "American Street: The American Dream and the Immigrant Imagination," Ibi Zoboi presentation at Vanderbilt University (2019)
- *American Street* (2017) by Ibi Zoboi

OBJECTIVES

Discussion: Compare prior knowledge about a place (from books, lessons, or misinformation in the media) to experiences from authentic voices.

Text Analysis: Analyze how an author uses dialogue and revealing actions to reveal how a character exhibits resourcefulness, resilience, and recovery.

Writing: Brainstorm visual representations of a character's words and actions, and their impact on your life.

OPENING DISCUSSION

At the beginning of her presentation at Vanderbilt University, author Ibi Zoboi says:

> I had a very cerebral lecture prepared for a college visit that is very intellectual in terms of talking about Haiti from the Voodoo spiritual narrative and what it means to retain that narrative in the face of failed American Dreams so the horror part of it is when people come from a broken country or the poorest country in the Western Hemisphere to move to even poorer cities in the United States and the kind of horrors that immigrants confront. What does that mean from a mythological and spiritual standpoint? But we're not gonna go there because we're educators and I'm going to share the presentation that I share with young people and make it more personal. What I realized after doing both lectures over the past couple of years is it's easy to frame Haiti within an intellectual framework, meaning Haiti is an idea, Haitian history is an idea, Haitian people are an idea, but I rarely hear or see people talk about Haiti from a very personal perspective in that I'm someone from Haiti. I'm an immigrant.
>
> [minutes 2:09–3:16]

Invite students to discuss what they know of Haiti and how that knowledge compares to what Ibi Zoboi shared in this introduction to her talk.

TEXT ANALYSIS

Show students the publisher's book summary of *American Street* (2017) by Ibi Zoboi and ask students to think about the following guiding question as they look at two excerpts from the first two chapters of the book.

Guiding Question: How does Ibi Zoboi use dialogue and actions to reveal a character's resourcefulness, resilience, and recovery?

Support students in their analysis by having them color-code what they notice the author doing in these excerpts. (When are characters speaking with others? When are characters sharing internal thinking? When are characters showing physical action?)

Excerpt #1 from Chapter 1:

"Is she being detained?"

I stare and blink and shake my head. I search my brain for this word, trying to find the Creole word for it, or a French one—*détenir*: to hold back, to keep from moving ...

"I can't help. You've been standing here all this time and your luggage is still at baggage claim. Now, follow the signs to pick up your things. I'm sure you have family waiting for you." She speaks slowly, as if I am stupid.

I purse my lips and clench my fists. How do I tell her that I am not going to the other side without Manman? How do I say that my mother has not seen her big sister, Matant Majorie, since they were teenagers and Manman wanted nothing more than to hold her face and plant a big wet kiss on her cheek? But the English words don't come as fast as the many Creole insults at the tip of my tongue for this Deborah Howard. (p. 4)

Excerpt #2 from Chapter 2:

"Fabiola, my mother is gonna handle it, all right? She's the one who sent for you both in the first place. She'll make a few phone calls, and before you know it, your mom will be here." Chantal's voice is candy—sweet but firm.

She takes off her thick, long scarf and wraps it around my shoulders—a gesture that only my mother has ever done for me. Back in Haiti, it was always just me and Manman. But now, my world has ballooned and in it are these three cousins, and my aunt, too. Family takes care of each other, I tell myself. We will get my manman.

We leave the airport. It feels like I'm leaving part of me behind—a leg, an arm. My whole heart. (pp. 12–13)

WRITING

Begin this part by asking students to think of a person in their lives who exhibits resourcefulness, resilience, and recovery. This can be a loved one, a friend, an adult they admire in their school or community, or a character they've read about in their classes. This can also be an artist, activist, athlete, entrepreneur, or any other figure in their lives that exhibits these characteristics.

Ask students to sketch out a visual representation of this person's characteristics. This sketch might look like one of the following:

- A web with what this person has said and done
- A scene from this character's life

Students can wrap up this part of the lesson by selecting one line or image from their sketch to write a letter of gratitude to that person, acknowledging what they've said, what they've done, and the impact their words and actions have had in their lives.

CLOSING DISCUSSION

Return to the "American Street: The American Dream and the Immigrant Imagination" talk by Ibi Zoboi at Vanderbilt University (2019), particularly to the question-and-answer part [minutes 44:33–46:33] on Zoboi's mother not speaking Creole to her and Zoboi's understanding of Blackness. What does Zoboi mean by "I did not feel comfortable until I embraced a global Blackness"?

TESTIMONIO: Brendaly Torres

K-12 Culturally Responsive Educator for the Bronx, New York City Public Schools

I met Brendaly when she was teaching at East Bronx Academy for the Future in the Bronx, New York. I was a literacy consultant at the school, and we planned several literacy units together. I remember reading Huey P. Newton's *Revolutionary Suicide* memoir and planning with Brendaly. I'm so grateful more students and teachers get to learn with her!

BRENDALY ON HER JOURNEY AS AN EDUCATOR:

Before I even started teaching, I was an in-class tutor at East Bronx Academy for the Future. I was in undergrad, obtaining my sociology degree, and my dream was to become a lawyer. But the more time I spent at East Bronx Academy for the Future I actually just felt like I found my niche ... I started subbing, and I was initially teaching Math for ELLs [English Language Learners] … I got to work with people who have similar backgrounds to me or similar backgrounds to people in my family. I, too, learned English in school, so that connection just continued to build. While having my sub license, I signed up for Lehman College [City University of New York], and I applied to their TESOL program … My days were super tight because I would go from teaching all day, then I ran the after-school program for ELLs, and then at night, I would go to school until about ten o'clock at night and then do it all over again.

During my time there, I taught Math, Sociology, and Newcomer English as a New Language for grades 6 through 12. I also had to coteach with different grade levels. I also cotaught in Science, Global History, and U.S. History. I really was very lucky to be able to tap into different subjects which just have really helped my students because I was able to be in all the classes with them, and I could help them build on those connections.

I was there for thirteen years, and through my time there, I became a teacher leader. I began instructional coaching, and after thirteen years of being there, I went to an International School for four years, where I was the literacy through ENL [English as a New Language] teacher. I was also a team leader/teacher leader. I was part of the ILT [Instructional Leadership Team]. And then, after four years of being at the High School level of Internationals, I went into Middle School. There I was an instructional coach/ENL teacher for seventh grade and team leader.

I just finished my Advanced Certificate in School Building and School District Leadership. The biggest change is … the more I got into teaching, the more I learned about culturally responsive education and making sure that we embed supports to build access for all students and foster an inclusive environment. I think that sometimes we think we know what will work, but as you are learning, you also start unlearning. So, even the style and the way that I teach are so different from when I first started. I used to have this idea that students had to read a seven-page paper or an entire book to learn something, but by embedding more videos and discussions, that's gonna give the students the same information. This allows them to access material in a better way and really push their thinking by removing what can be a daunting task.

BRENDALY ON HER FIRST MEMORY SEEING HERSELF AS A WRITER:

It was my seventh-grade poetry unit, and I hated poetry… or so I thought. Here is where I discovered that I actually really loved poetry, but I think I was so used to seeing one style of poetry. It was then that I just got access to different styles of poetry and that just opened me up and really helped me express myself. That was the first time I saw myself as a writer, and also the teacher had us perform poems and I was really anxious about it. But I practiced, and I did all the things. I don't remember the poem but it was an Ode to Oreos.

BRENDALY ON HER FAVORITE WRITING ACTIVITY WITH LATINX TEENS:

One of my favorite writing prompts is that I will loop an instrumental, could be a beat. I tend to go a lot with Bad Bunny instrumentals in the background. I'll loop it twice, and on the board, I'll put an open-ended type of writing prompt. For example, "what is your favorite__________?" And then it could be your favorite anything. I feel like that really invites students to kind of play with words. Have them really think, and not have to be so confined to things like, what's your favorite ice cream, or what's your favorite picture, this allows for students to push their creativity when leaving it open-ended because it allows for them to think and write freely and also gives the teacher input to where they are as writers. So when you leave it open-ended like that, it really helps them expand and write.

BRENDALY ON LATINX AUTHORS GIVING HER LIFE RIGHT NOW:

I'm gonna go with *When We Make It* [by Elisabet Velasquez]. It's a novel written in verse, and one of the reasons why I liked it is because I connected to the book so much. A lot of the themes in the book just reminded me of me growing up. Even though the book takes place in Brooklyn, and I grew up in the Bronx, I was able to make connections with the characters and what they were dealing with. Some of the battles that they were fighting I also fought at similar times in my life. For my students, it being a novel in verse made them apprehensive at first, but the writing and themes got them talking and opening up in a way about some serious topics that provided a safe space to open up and be vulnerable. I do not think that I could have done that with another book. Meeting the author and having her come in was a major plus. She spoke like us and wrote like us, and that provided a connection that was really impactful, and it just made you want to keep reading. For a lot of them it was the first time seeing an author, but not only seeing an author, having someone that they could connect to linguistically and culturally was huge.

BRENDALY'S ADVICE FOR WRITING TEACHERS OF LATINX YOUTH:

I feel like creative writing is where you get the most impact from kids. And it really gives you the information that you need in order to help kids move forward. So, focusing more on creative writing and really bringing the kids in the writing … It's all about progress and process. And that takes time.

BRENDALY ON WRITING SHE'S WORKING ON NOW:

I've actually been working on a book for a few years now, and I feel like I pick it up just when I need to. Right now, I'm getting the itch to pick it up again. It's in very skeleton mode, but it lives in a notebook … It would be for a middle-grade or young-adult audience. [My writing mentor] would be my friend Elisabet Velasquez. She pushes me a lot. She gives me homework. I'm secretly rolling my eyes 'cause that's our running joke, "I'm like, are you giving me homework again?" She's like, "of course, I'm giving you homework again." So she has been a pillar, really pushing me to focus on my writing again because I think that we sometimes fall into [thoughts] like, "can I really do this? Should I put this out there? How much should I put out there?" She's been helping me a lot with that.

Chapter Six

In the Heights: Communities That Elevate, Communities That Stifle

"I'm from Long Island, so I'm sure you know how that is over there. Growing up was very different. My Spanish teacher was a white woman ... I grew up wanting to be that typical white girl ... I wasn't really proud of who I was, and now I've learned to make

it my major. I think I saw the change start to happen towards the end of high school and entering into college, I was working more with bilingual children, and I noticed that I got along with them better when I did speak Spanish, and it just started to make me feel like, oh wait, this is something I could help other people with ... I don't think I told anyone that I felt like different, but I do think it was internal. I definitely think taking the PRLS [Puerto Rican Latinx Studies at Brooklyn College] courses here has helped, and it has opened [me] up to, like, wow, there are actually Latino writers, and it had me Googling Guatemalan writers ... I definitely think coming to Brooklyn College and seeing how that it's an actual major, because this major isn't offered everywhere."

—**Melanie, undergraduate Childhood Education with a Bilingual Extension, Puerto Rican and Latinx Studies Minor**

What does feeling like you belong and are nurtured in a community mean? We'd hope youth would feel welcomed in all spaces within school and outside of school and that, when they are not, they are supported in crafting their best exit strategies. I've been incredibly moved by the young people who show us how they keep each other afloat in the midst of what seem to be insurmountable challenges. In doing so, they craft community in ways that may look different than some of us may have experienced in our teens. When a loved one experienced anxiety from attending a toxic school where racism, transphobia, and xenophobia ran rampant amongst the student and staff population, they shared with me that it was an online community that made them feel less alone. I witnessed this when students from the Puerto Rican Alliance (PRA, established on my campus in 1968 during the Civil Rights Movement) (Pérez y González, 2021) stood in solidarity with seventeen other student organizations in calling attention to Islamophobia and over-policing on campus during a faculty council meeting (one PRA member read the letter to the college president). These same communities of students weathered several storms while attempting to call attention to these issues and the injustices toward Palestinians in Gaza and those in the diaspora during on-campus and off-campus rallies. I saw a tremendous showing of solidarity at One Police Plaza in New York City after violent arrests on April 30, 2024 at City College of New York and Columbia University protests (PSCCUNY, 2024). Not a demonstration. Not a rally. Instead, just a physical presence outside of the police precinct waiting for people to be released. Community for these youth has gone from spaces on social media to physical places that encourage them to be their full selves, including expressing their questions and righteous rage on injustices often perpetuated by our own institutions.

In "Participating in the Divine with God on the Picket Line," Cuban American mujerista theologian Ada María Isasi-Díaz begins by recounting her experience while protesting apartheid outside the South African embassy (2001). I've been thinking a lot about this piece, returning to it often as a form of meditation in the past year as protests call attention to the apartheid experienced by Palestinian people for decades. Before my bilingual education studies at Hunter College, City University of New York, I attended Princeton Theological Seminary for a master's in Divinity, focusing on religion and society. I can't emphasize enough the impact that Ada María Isasi-Díaz's writing and mujerista theology had on my life as a Latina and recovering evangelical Christian. Leaving that evangelical community and immersing myself in graduate studies on Latin American liberation theology and mujerista theology movements provided me with a different vision of what community could be when we center the lives of those who've been relegated to the margins by the powerful in society.

Like Isasi-Díaz, most of my students are most certainly in profound community with one another. I'm grateful Melanie (as you can see from the chapter's opening quote) has found a community at the college and in Ethnic Studies, and that, in turn, she's found a sense of self. I think about the reciprocity that is required of community and what drives us in our relationships as we consider how best to create these experiences for Latinx youth. Isasi-Díaz (2001) ends her piece with:

> All true love requires the give and take of relationships and this is what spirituality is: the give and take of my relationship with God, which has to be something concrete. Such concreteness becomes a reality in our love for one another, an incarnated love that is passionate, that calls us to engage each other, to share ourselves with each other. For me, this is what spirituality is all about.

Whether we believe in the divine as a being, several beings, something within us, or something in our interaction with other beings (including the Earth), I hope this sense of reciprocity of "incarnated love" drives our community relations. I wrote the following poems and personal narrative from that tension between a mourning of what could've been when I was a teen navigating community and a glimmering sense of hope, one that playwright Tony Kushner shared with students at my campus at the end of his "Writing for Life" conversation (Ethyle R. Wolfe Institute,

2024), expressing that students' activism is what drives him these days, providing him that motivation to get up in the morning.

Who or what motivates you to continue teaching? How do the communities in your life sustain your advocacy for Latinx youth? When I was a high school student, my church communities gave me the opportunity to develop my translation and singing skills. You would find me on the stage at the United Palace Theater in Washington Heights on Sundays as the pastor's interpreter for his sermons (that meant hours of navigating my Chilean Spanish with his Dominican Spanish and English translations) and as a singer in the church's ministry group (another hour of singing in Spanish). I often joke with friends who let me know about concerts at this theater (famous Latinx artists perform there) that I sang there first!

Yet there came a time when I had to part ways and find a new community because the church leaders who had welcomed my family and me and given us opportunities to share in so much of life with them began spewing such hatred from the pulpit—from homophobic sermons to judgments on low-income families for not giving the church the money that they were asking (thank you gospel of prosperity and mega churches for the examples). My parents and I were horrified. I had stepped away from all leadership positions (including translating) at that time and watched as the church that was once about helping the community became about displays of wealth and shutting (certain) people out.

By day, I'd hang out with all kinds of young adults at my college's Commuter Commons, where I found a different community of NYU students who didn't dorm, so we'd take the train into campus and needed a place to connect (and warm up our food in a microwave because everything was so expensive around there). Unlike Melanie's journey, I had this crisis of self and faith because I thought I had found my people to help me through the next stage in my life (college), but I had to start over because I couldn't reconcile the reciprocity and love that I witnessed by day on my college campus in Commuter Commons (and later the NYU Gospel Choir that I joined) with the messages of *selective* love from my church.

Poem: "I Was Told to Leave 'All That Multicultural Work' for My 'Urban' Schools"

That reality of facing messages of love and acceptance that seem more conditional and selective than comprehensive of everyone is something I continue facing in my life. I wrote about this in my poem "I Was Told to Leave 'All that Multicultural Work' for My 'Urban' Schools," when one of my supervisors at a literacy organization called me aside to share feedback from a school I visited in Chappaqua,

Singing at a church in the Bronx, New York

New York, in my role as a literacy consultant. I had hoped that this would be a supportive community, not just for sharing resources at different schools but also for people like me, interested in nurturing young people's reading and writing lives through culturally and linguistically sustaining children's literature. I think back to this moment often, questioning when leaders in education do not support education experts, especially those from minoritized communities. This moment was a turning point in my life as I had been trying to suppress those feelings that crept up when I worked for a predominantly white organization: frustration, despair, and rage. I spent so much energy trying to effect change from within while also finding ways to be accepted. It was exhausting. I believe Toni Morrison said it best:

> The function, the very serious function of racism, is distraction. It keeps you from doing your work. It keeps you explaining, over and over again, your reason for being. Somebody says you have no language, and you spend twenty years proving that you do.
> (Portland State University, 1975)

The personal narrative that follows this poem is an example of people doing the work and not having to explain their reason for being. They just exist in a space that is already accepting and with people who support them in thriving. I paired the poem and the narrative to show that reality.

I Was Told to Leave "All That Multicultural Work" for My "Urban" Schools

"Just leave out that multicultural work,"
you said with that privileged
white-woman-kind-of-confidence,
the kind I saw as a college senior
when I reunited with my high school mentor
and at the end of our dinner, she asked,
"Did you reach out to me because you need money?"

A lifetime of preparation, experience, and skills
wouldn't be enough to be accepted.
"El mejor regalo que le podemos dejar es la educación,"
mamá's reminder at each stage in my life.
But how many degrees does a Latina need to be taken seriously
in a white supremacist society?

You would've thought I got my Ph.D. in respectability politics.
Soul-cycled gatherings.
J. Crew-ed out in structured dresses.
Minimized my soul
while limiting my use of Spanish.
Listened to your stories of summer homes
and how you saw the needs of those kids in urban schools.

Was it the Spanish in Gloria Anzaldúa's
"How to Tame a Wild Tongue"
or Jacqueline Woodson's Black girl protagonist
in *The Other Side* read aloud
that shook you?
Or was it my existence as an expert in these spaces that you
could not accept?

Like the white woman educator from Staten Island who interrupted
my keynote at Teachers College, Columbia University—
"But you're not presenting both sides!"—when I talked
Black Lives Matter

(and you asked me to write an apology to them and others who said
I was too political when talking about education)
Your racism is showing.

—and I'm not
apologizing.

Personal Narrative: "Latinx Teacher Retreat"

Boston-bred, Chicago-based Jewish and Mexican-American organizer, activist and poet Jonathan Mendoza (2019) said the following as he considered his response when asked about the source of his hope:

> I recently attended an event at which Janna Jihad, a 13-year-old Palestinian activist and the youngest certified journalist in the world, recounted words frequently uttered in the Palestinian liberation movement: "Palestine will be free." The statement was not the more common: "Free Palestine." It was not a plea; it was not a demand. It was a prophecy. If I am to have hope for, and belief in, a future where we are all free, it is because young people do.

Mendoza goes on to share that the organizing work is both external (protests) and internal (healing through art). Mendoza's essay (2019) and his work on housing justice in Chicago reminded me of the connections I made with the Rise Home Stories Project for the *Alejandria Fights Back!/ ¡La lucha de Alejandria!* picture book (Hernández Linares & Rise Home Stories Project, 2021). There are kind and brilliant people working on the ground with communities to make sure people have their right to housing, and particularly with Mendoza's work, amplifying youth voice and power. I often think of what it means to listen to our youth and their call for freedom, especially with their involvement in mass social justice movements.

While I attended high school, I had the beautiful opportunity to engage local youth through my church's "Each One Teach One" Saturday program. We had homework support, English classes, trips, music sessions, and more! We met at our church in the Bronx by Lehman College, a few blocks from the 4 train, making it accessible for so many of us who came from across New York City. We would then connect across the week either at church services at the United Palace Theater in Washington Heights, at Riverside Park, or any other public space where we'd set up with our food (there was always great Dominican and Puerto Rican food shared) and sometimes with microphones and instruments (you could often find me on the corner of 175th and Broadway by El Malecón, singing or inviting folks to the church services). That community meant so much to me at a time when my parents were doing much of the same. They loved meeting with families, especially newly arrived immigrants looking for places and people to make them feel less alone.

In Mendoza's poem "Confessions on Gratitude" (Button Poetry, 2018), I learned of the communities that shaped Mendoza's ancestry: Jewish from Russia, Poland, and Spain, and Chihuahua, Mexico. I am moved to reflect on what I get access to as a (now) documented citizen living in the United States, as a speaker of English and Spanish, and as someone with multiple graduate degrees. I recognize that these privileges grant me access and a greater responsibility to make space for those who aren't granted a seat at the table.

The personal narrative that follows presents a counter-narrative, a moment with Latina education leaders facilitating a retreat for Latina teachers in a teacher preparation program at Kennesaw State University, Georgia. I weave in the description of the sounds and sights of that pre-service teacher retreat, along with my emotions witnessing that mentorship and cariño from education leaders who come from that community and work so hard to cultivate more Latine educators. I present the poem in this chapter and the narrative that follows because they mirror a frequent experience of those of us who navigate different communities where we aren't listened to at one moment but, in the other, we're surrounded by people who hear us and create spaces for all of us to shine.

LATINX TEACHER RETREAT

"Como la flor (como la flor), con tanto amor, me diste tú, se marchitó." Selena's "Como la Flor" lyrics boom from the projector's speakers, and I feel at home. I sing away (as one does when Selena is on). At the sign-in table, I see my coauthored book *En Comunidad: Lessons for Centering the Voices and Experiences of Bilingual Latinx Students* along with Prisca Dorcas Mojica Rodríguez's *For Brown Girls with Sharp Edges and Tender Hearts* and the picture book *Spanish is the Language of My Family* by Michael Genhart, illustrated by John Parra. It's the first time I've seen my book partnered with these other books, and I take a deep breath to take it all in. How wonderful that these undergraduate Latinx students, all future teachers, would get copies of these books!

I walk around the room and notice the markers, journals, stickers, and craft supplies. Prof. Sanjuana Rodríguez, Prof. Paula Guerra, and psychologist and guest speaker Karla Montgomery-Ramirez start setting up the extra craft supplies for the activity in the next room where the breakfast and interviews would be hosted (Kennesaw State University is collecting data on these students' experiences). "¿De qué parte de Colombia?" I ask Karla about Colombia and share how much I miss visiting family in her beautiful country.

Students start arriving and I'm introduced to each. I had spent the previous days in meals and on campus events with Prof. Sanjuana Rodríguez and her colleague, Prof. Paula Guerra, so I was already familiar with their work, but nothing prepared me for the showering of cariño by the faculty and the students for each other. There were hugs and laughs as students and professors started catching up.

After I'm introduced, I begin with the following Cherrie Moraga (2011) quote:

> I write to remember.
> I make rite (ceremony) to remember.
> It is my right to remember.

I talk about ritual and community, my Chilean roots, and my very New York education journey. I get to know the students after we read the poem "Gate A-4" (2008) by Palestinian poet Naomi Shihab Nye. "How would you end this poem?" I ask them to use Nye's framing:

> This is the world I want to live in.
> The ______ world.
> Not a single person ______.
> about ______.
> This can still happen ______.
> Not everything is lost.

In place of Nye's "shared" world from the first blank, students had words such as: "safe," "just," and "peaceful." It was a wonderful and profound way to get to know this future teacher community. I then walk them through some excerpts from the picture book *Growing an Artist: The Story of a Landscaper and His Son* (2022) by John Parra. One of the undergraduate students talks about her personal connection with this book: her father is a landscaper and has the same name as a character in the book! Another student talks about the impact of including that rejection from the classmate who ignores John and his dad when they are working on the landscaping at his home. We talk about the shame around working-class jobs and how we've witnessed that in our lives. The room has about five small round tables, and some deep conversations are happening at each. I take my time walking to each table as I carry a copy of the book in Spanish and English while I leave one of the spreads projected on the screen.

Although my time was short with them, I was most impacted by the space that the professors created because, after my facilitation, teachers had psychologist Karla Montgomery-Ramirez walk them through walking meditation and a collage activity. They culminated the session with a book club discussion on Prisca Dorcas Mojica

Rodríguez's book. Not only were the students sharing passages that resonated with them, but they were also honest with the tensions they were holding, all feelings the book was helping them process. "She sounds so angry," the first student shared and then expanded on what they do with the anger in their life. Others responded by summarizing the reasons for that anger, pulling quotes on white supremacy and the connections they felt with the author as Latinx immigrants. Like Nye, "this is the world I want to live in," (2008) the world where Latinx teachers are embraced from their undergrad studies, with the questions and discomforts around their identities and curriculum, all through their teaching journey.

Leaving a church youth group event in the Bronx, New York

TEACHER TEXT SET

1. Media (podcasts):
   a. *Latino USA*
   b. *Latino Rebels Radio*
   c. *Tamarindo*
   d. *The Latino Majority*: "Sylvia Acevedo: Engineering Two Solutions" episode
2. Articles:
   a. CNN "Opinion: The next Census Could Reveal a Very Different America" by Cristian Arroyo-Santiago
   b. "How Latino Congregations are Transforming Communities: A Survey Report" by The Brown Church Institute, Fuller Centro Latino and Urban Strategies
   c. "Black and Latinx NYC Public High School Students Win Expanded Sports Team Access with Proposed Settlement in Sports Equity Class Action Lawsuit" news release
3. Books:
   a. *Living Beyond Borders: Growing Up Mexican in America* edited by Margarita Longoria
   b. *Wild Tongues Can't Be Tamed: 15 Voices from the Latinx Diaspora* edited by Saraciea J. Fennell
   c. *An African American and Latinx History of the United States* by Paul Ortiz
   d. *Finding Latinx: In Search of the Voices Redefining Latino Identity* by Paola Ramos
4. Museum resources:
   a. Smithsonian American Art Museum Arte Latine/ Latinx Art Teacher Resources
   b. Smithsonian National Museum of the American Latino
5. Films:
   a. *Spare Parts*
   b. *Underwater Dreams*
6. Recommended youth organizations and social media accounts:
   a. Girls for Gender Equity: @GGENYC
   b. The Brotherhood Sister Sol: @brosis512
   c. Dream Yard: @dream_yard

LESSON SEQUENCE OVERVIEW AND STUDENT TEXT SET In the Heights: Communities That Elevate, Communities That Stifle			
Lesson #1	**Lesson #2**	**Lesson #3**	**Lesson #4**
In the Heights film opening scene *In the Heights* interviews with writer and producer Quiara Alegría Hudes and actors Leslie Grace and Gregory Diaz IV	"No existe un mundo poshuracán: Puerto Rican Art in the Wake of Hurricane María" Whitney Museum of American Art YouTube video "the independence (of puerto rico)" / "la independencia (de puerto rico)" by Roque Raquel Salas Rivera "Chicago Poet José Olivarez: Straddling Two Cultures and How It's Impacted His Art" on *La Vida Baseball* YouTube channel "No Time to Wait" by José Olivarez	"Interview with Author Letisha Marrero" on the *Women of Color Read, Too* blog *Salsa Magic* by Letisha Marrero Dominican Writers Association "Letisha Marrero Brings Us on a Spiritual Journey in *Salsa Magic*"	"When We Make It: Meet Author Elisabet Velasquez" Penguin Teens video *When We Make It* by Elisabet Velasquez

Lesson #1: In the Heights: Communities That Elevate, Communities That Stifle: A Multimodal Introduction

I'll never forget the epic fail of a lesson, or what a mentor would encourage me to call a "teachable moment." I had recently watched *The Golden Compass* film that was based on the book and thought this would be a great whole-class read! The film was released during my first year of teaching, and I was eager to continue building on the momentum from our initial community-building experience with a book. We had read, discussed, and written about *The Color of My Words* (*El color de mis palabras*) (2001) by Lynn Joseph, and students loved the book and the experience of following a book in English and in Spanish as a class and in small book club discussions. What I hadn't accounted for was that I was into this next book and film and didn't know if the interest was mutual with my sixth graders. In retrospect, I also should've asked the literacy coach for support with analyzing reading and writing data to see if the book would've been a match at that time of the school year. As soon as I started the read-aloud and talked about writing craft, I had lost most of the class.

Fast forward to over a decade later, and I'm one of two middle-grade deans and teaching two middle-grade English classes at an independent school in New York State. Instead of making assumptions with a text as I did during my first year of teaching, I decided to do more listening this time and learn more about my students' interests. Two of my seventh-grade students come up to me during our morning snack time, stepping away from their Four-Square games to tell me about *In the Heights* (Chu et al., 2021). They loved the film and began telling me about the plot, acting, singing, and dancing. Our quick snack break was over too soon, and we all had to make our way to class. This lesson is inspired by that conversation with the students and my love of musical theater, along with the brilliant journalists who are featured below.

WRITING LESSON #1

LESSON TEXTS

- *In the Heights* film opening scene
- *In the Heights* interviews with writer and producer Quiara Alegría Hudes and actors Leslie Grace and Gregory Diaz IV

OBJECTIVES

Discussion: Discuss the characteristics of different Latinx communities as presented in popular media.

Text Analysis: Compare how different scenes from one text present a varied view of Latinidad.

Writing: Write a script that follows an opening musical scene in a film.

OPENING DISCUSSION

Invite students to discuss their observations of the opening scene from *In the Heights* (Chu et al., 2021) film (available on the Warner Bros. Pictures YouTube channel as "In the Heights - First 8 Minutes"). What is the setting? Who lives there? What do they see and hear? How do the camera angles change, and what do they reveal?

TEXT ANALYSIS

Explain to students that they will engage in a jigsaw activity for the text analysis, focusing with a group that watches one series' clip, followed by a discussion with a group that has watched two different series' clips. Whether or not students have seen the *In the Heights* film, the following clip and corresponding quotes will help them begin to think about the guiding question: How are Latinx communities represented in this text? If students need more support, you can begin by having them observe *who* is represented, *what* experiences are highlighted, and *what narratives are missing* from the text.

In the Heights commentaries by actors:

1. Nina (played by Leslie Grace) returns home: Watch the PBS News Hour interview "Leslie Grace on How *In the Heights* Brings Crucial Latinx Stories to the Screen" (PBS News Hour, 2021).
2. Sonny's undocumented status is revealed: See the *Entertainment Weekly* (Jones, 2021) and *Teen Vogue* interviews (Villa, 2021).

Regarding the first clip, Quiara Alegría Hudes, *In the Heights* writer and producer, says the following about Nina's character compared to her own life in an *Entertainment Weekly* interview:

> With Nina, there's a lot I relate to in her because in my house, I was the first generation to go to college … After we opened on Broadway, a lot of the elite, very expensive private tuition schools changed their financial aid packages so that there was less focus on loans and more focus on scholarship. There was still a tremendous uphill battle for families … but it gave me this opportunity to dig deeper and go farther into what are the other challenges Nina faces while she's at school. I rewrote her specifically to be Afro-Latina. And what she experiences when she gets there is not just financial hardship, but also these microaggressions—that at times, whether she's welcomed in that space comes into question.
>
> (Jones, 2021)

At the end of *In the Heights*, viewers do not get a resolution for Sonny's status. Hudes states the following regarding this decision as the writer and one of the producers: "I feel that it's stronger as an open question," and that "It's up to us who do have the privilege of citizenship to decide what Sonny's future is" (Soerens, 2021).

When asked about the undocumented plot in the film and how it's "not necessarily an issue that gets applied as much to a lot of Latinos, specifically in New York City," by Marcus Jones for *Entertainment Weekly*, Hudes responds:

> Well, the demographic reality of Washington Heights is that it is predominantly Dominican. So it is really present as an urgent issue in the community … us Puerto Ricans, spiritually, emotionally, culture-wise, and linguistically, we are immigrants … And so in some ways I think it almost puts the responsibility more on us to step up to the plate for our brothers and sisters in the community who face challenges in that regard.
>
> (Jones, 2021)

Gregory Diaz IV, the actor who plays Sonny, said the following in a *Teen Vogue* interview about his role in representing the undocumented community:

> "That was something they added on after the first script," Gregory reveals. "It was a conversation that we had just wanting it as not something that defined him, but it does exist there and does put regulations on his life because ultimately Sonny just wants to be able to grow up and do big things. As an actor playing this undocumented person, it was something that I wanted to help uplift and show in a positive sense."
>
> (Villa, 2021)

WRITING

Share with students the following storytelling/writing tip from Lin Manuel-Miranda:

> For me, it always gets back to story. And I think if you set out to say: "I'm going to write a poem about the injustice of voter fraud. I'm going to write a musical about voter fraud and rigged elections," and I'm telling you it's going to be boring. It's going to be boring because you're starting with themes instead of with the story. I fell in love with Hamilton's story, and in chasing his story it allowed me to write about all these other themes because they're inherent in his life. The notion of power. The notion of the immigrant narrative, and how immigrant has positive connotations in our society just as often as it has negative connotations in our society. And how it can be used as both an aspirational word and an epithet in politics. There are the notions of who gets to make the decisions in our century and the limits of representational democracy. If I set out to write a show about that, it would be so boring. But if I'm writing about Hamilton and his friend Burr, and Burr gets locked out of

> a dinner, suddenly we can talk about all that stuff and it's exciting because the personal is political.
>
> (Nieman Foundation for Journalism at Harvard, 2016)

Invite students to write the script for a scene that would follow the opening musical scene they watched at the beginning of this lesson. Students can consider some of the following components for their script of one scene:

- Action lines
- Character names
- Dialogue descriptions
- Dialogue

This should be a fun exploration of their imagination and what they know of the story so far. For more support, students can view a page from the *In the Heights* screenplay available online (this of course is more developed but shows the action lines, character names, dialogue descriptions, and dialogue). If they've already experienced the musical or film, students can bring that knowledge to the script of a scene by considering what they'd keep and what they'd change in their version.

CLOSING DISCUSSION

Option #1: You can continue with the same text, *In the Heights*, by showing some clips or excerpts from sources that provide commentary on some of the topics students discussed in the text analysis earlier as a whole class or ones that were brought up in their small groups. For example, Felice León (The Root, 2021) addresses the erasure of Afro-Latinxs from *In the Heights* or the different experiences of the actors revealed in the African American Film Critics Association (AAFCA) Virtual Roundtable: *In the Heights* Interview (The AAFCA Channel, 2021).

Option #2: Students can compare the opening scene from the *In the Heights* (Chu et al., 2021) film (available on the Warner Bros. Pictures YouTube channel as "In the Heights - First 8 Minutes") with any scene from a series by and about a Latinx community, such as *Gentefied, One Day at a Time* and *Gordita Chronicles*. What are the similarities? Differences? What comes up in articles about these series, especially comments on why they were all canceled?

Option #3: Students can meet in small groups to share and rehearse their scripts. They can make plans as to what they'd like to do with those scenes: return to them during free time or theater/art time, prepare a class performance for the school or other grades, and/or prepare a special performance and panel discussion on the film/musical's themes for an evening with families.

Lesson #2: In the Heights: Communities That Elevate, Communities That Stifle: Poetry

Growing up in New York meant missing out on all the milestones from my extended family while at the same time making friends from different parts of the world at my schools in Queens and Manhattan. Although we spoke different languages with our families and some of us had different faith traditions, we understood the plight of immigrants and the pressures as first-generation students when we were applying to colleges. Whether my high school best friends were from Indonesia, Mexico, Puerto Rico, Ecuador, or the Dominican Republic, we had similar upbringings with families that made sacrifices for us to be where we were at. Another pattern across our experiences was the assumptions people made about people who were from our families' homelands or the stereotypes they had about us as teens from those places.

The poems "the independence (of puerto rico)" / "la independencia (de puerto rico)" by Roque Raquel Salas Rivera and "No Time to Wait" by José Olivarez address both the comebacks to the degrading comments and the gratitude and pride we feel in the connections to the communities that sustain us. I had the beautiful opportunity to see my undergraduate students' reactions to Roque Raquel Salas Rivera's poems when they walked through the Whitney Museum exhibition "No existe un mundo poshuracán: Puerto Rican Art in the Wake of Hurricane María." The exhibition's title is from a line in one of their poems from the book *While They Sleep: Under the Bed Is Another Country* (2019). That same year, Denice Ocana, one of my undergraduate students majoring in Psychology and taking Puerto Rican and Latinx Studies courses, presented the poetry of José Olivarez. It was the first time the rest of the class had read Olivarez and I loved that a student introduced them to his work.

WRITING LESSON #2

LESSON TEXTS

- "No existe un mundo poshuracán: Puerto Rican Art in the Wake of Hurricane María" Whitney Museum of American Art YouTube video (2022)
- "the independence (of puerto rico)" / "la independencia (de puerto rico)" by Roque Raquel Salas Rivera (2020)
- "No Time to Wait" by José Olivarez (2023)
- "Chicago Poet José Olivarez: Straddling Two Cultures and How It's Impacted His Art" on La Vida Baseball YouTube channel (2019)

OBJECTIVES

Discussion: Understand how artists are informed by their communities and how their art shapes communities.

Text Analysis: Analyze how poetry can be a counter-narrative on different communities as conveyed by people within those communities.

Writing: Select from two different poetry structures to write a poem about a community.

OPENING DISCUSSION

Show students the video "No existe un mundo poshuracán: Puerto Rican Art in the Wake of Hurricane María" on the Whitney Museum of American Art YouTube channel. This was a momentous exhibition, the first of its kind to showcase Puerto Rican art in a major U.S. museum in almost fifty years. Students will meet poet Roque Raquel Salas Rivera in this video and learn how their poetry informed the exhibition's name.

Show students the first five minutes of "Chicago Poet José Olivarez: Straddling Two Cultures and How It's Impacted His Art" (2019) on the *La Vida Baseball* YouTube channel.

Ask students to discuss how the poets' and artists' communities inform their art.

TEXT ANALYSIS

Read Roque Raquel Salas Rivera's poem "the independence (of puerto rico)" / "la independencia (de puerto rico)" (2020) and invite students to comment on the changes in the poem. Notice how the poem flows from "we are ..." with adjectives that describe Puerto Ricans to "they tell us ...," continues with "we are" and ends with the word "beauty." Have students first identify the adjectives used by the poet to describe themself and Puerto Ricans ("fiercer," "bigger," "braver," etc.) and those that are used to describe how others perceive them and other Puerto Ricans. What is the difference? Why does it matter to note that difference? If students need more support with answering the latter, they can return to the video clip from the opening discussion that addressed the need to highlight this disparity in the Whitney Museum's exhibit "No existe un mundo poshuracán: Puerto Rican Art in the Wake of Hurricane María."

After students analyze Roque Raquel Salas Rivera's poem, ask them to do the same with José Olivarez's "No Time to Wait." This poem is from Olivarez's book *Promises of Gold* (2023), which has poems in English with a translation in Spanish by David Ruano González. Ask students to take a look at this poem through the lens of a counter-narrative on community. The previous poem had a counter-narrative on the Puerto Rican community. In this case, we have a counter-narrative on a community that supports immigrant families from Mexico. Poet and host of the *Poetry Unbound* podcast Pádraig Ó Tuama has the following to say about Olivarez's poem:

> So the "alone you might think," asks you to pause and to go: Really? Is that true? It asks you to choose to do a double-take. What else is true in the presence of an experience of aloneness and experience of newness upon newness? New to Chicago, new to the U.S., and perhaps also looking for protection. You look for protection when you might feel like you are somehow vulnerable or exposed. And it's asking you to do a double-take on that, too. Exposed, you might think. But actually no, you're surrounded with all of this support from other Mexican families in the community.
>
> (Ó Tuama, 2023)

WRITING

Roque Raquel Salas Rivera and José Olivarez provide us with perspectives on two different communities. They are dispelling the myths we learn about each of those communities in their own ways. Roque Raquel Salas Rivera says that their poem "dismantles the idea that Puerto Rico's biggest problem is its insularism" (Salas Rivera, 2020). Invite students to think of a community they belong to, one that has had an impact on their lives, or one that they have left. They can mirror the structure of "the independence (of puerto rico)" / "la independencia (de puerto rico)" or "No Time to Wait" to convey how they feel about this community and/or what others outside of the community think. If there is a beloved community in the student's life, you can ask them to write their poem in the form of a love letter. See the writing prompts below to support the writers who might need them:

- What adjectives would you use to describe your community?
- How do you see your community?
- How do others see your community?
- Think of a story or anecdote you'd like to tell about your community.

CLOSING DISCUSSION

José Olivarez shared the following in the *La Vida Baseball* (2019) conversation:

> It was when I started to go to public school in Cayumet City. The first time that I showed up to try and attend pre-kindergarten they wouldn't let me sign up for class, and it was because they didn't have any English Language Learner instructors, right. So my very first experience of trying to go to school in the United States was of being rejected, and it made me feel like there was something wrong with speaking Spanish, there was something wrong with being Mexican. It made me feel like my identity was a burden, my identity was a problem for other people.

Use this quote and the poetry from this lesson to discuss how these poets used their craft to speak about and shape their community. You can also focus on your school community. Who feels most at home? Who feels welcomed? What would a newcomer student like José experience in your school? What can be done to make the experience a positive one for new students and families from racialized and language-minoritized communities?

Lesson #3: In the Heights: Communities That Elevate, Communities That Stifle: Middle-Grade Fiction

My first year teaching middle grade, I had several students whose lives revolved around sports or the arts. I'm talking about games or performances on weekends, years of coaching, and families who would travel with them to their events. There was Randy the baseball player, Genesis the performer, and several others who came into my sixth-grade class already knowing their interests, already forming part of communities with shared interests. As a teacher, that was a joy to witness and also a challenge I took upon myself as I sought out texts and activities that would match that spark and engage them in the classroom. But that was not the case with all students. Not everyone had a space to be themselves or meet with other like-minded people, to be encouraged and to grow. For those students, I would connect with colleagues to find more support, invite guest speakers, show documentaries, and truly find any texts and experiences I could create not to leave them out. I taught in a middle school that had over ten partnerships and opportunities for students to connect with others, including chess and Broadway theater groups. That was actually what most impressed me when I first interviewed at that school! The school's library media specialist/grant writer handed me a double-sided sheet with the list of the school's partnerships. It is lovely to provide those opportunities, especially in a public-school setting where these are often missing because the focus goes to test preparation and the over-policing of children.

Salsa Magic (2023) by Letisha Marrero is the book I wish existed when I was in middle grade and when I taught middle grades to help me address questions on faith communities. In an interview with the Dominican Writers Association (2023), Marrero says the following about her book:

> It's a story that's been in my head for about 20 years now. I read a book from a Santería priestess, and I was so fascinated by it. I learned about all the Orishas and I said to myself, "Why don't I know about this? Why is this the first I'm hearing about this?"

Whether it is the first time hearing about this or doing research to try to understand and dispel misunderstandings, this book creates entry points for necessary conversations. Marrero wants "Latine kids, in particular, to know their history" and to "educate non-Latine people about our history beyond what they've seen portrayed on TV, which may be stereotypical or negative" (Castillo, 2023). I found that my book talks (as quick as a minute or so before embarking on a book club unit or a new topic of study) with my students were a lot of "know your history" through this story and "reject stereotypes." I'm thrilled to share this text with you so you can add it to your text set, one that can continue to grow with information on other communities we can learn from within the Latine diaspora.

WRITING LESSON #3

LESSON TEXTS

- "Interview with Author Letisha Marrero" on the *Women of Color Read, Too* blog
- *Salsa Magic* by Letisha Marrero
- Dominican Writers Association "Letisha Marrero Brings Us on a Spiritual Journey in *Salsa Magic*"

OBJECTIVES

Discussion: Consider the events, people, and texts that influence our writing lives.

Text Analysis: Analyze how tension within a community impacts a young teen protagonist.

Writing: Create a fan-fiction scene that builds on what we know about a character's motivations and challenges from the text's first chapter.

OPENING DISCUSSION

Ask students to read and discuss the interview with Author Letisha Marrero on the *Women of Color Read, Too* blog (Ms. WOC Reads, 2024). Use the following questions to facilitate the discussion:

- What were the turning points in the author's writing life?
- How do these compare to the turning points in your life as a writer?
- What events, which people, and which texts have impacted you the most as you think about your approach to writing?

TEXT ANALYSIS

Invite students to look for the ways a community comes together during challenges and how it can grow to do better by all members of the community. For example, in this book that centers around a Puerto Rican family and Café Taza, specifically on the character of Maya and her mysterious/outcast aunt's visit from Puerto Rico, we see the beauty and the pain of communities that are there for one another but not all of the time. See how this rings true with the descriptions of the challenges in the excerpts from Chapter 1 below. While gentrification leads the family not to give up and to continue to serve their Mami's food, Titi Yaya's visit leads to Abuela telling the kids to stay away from this family member (who practices a different faith tradition). How does this tension (with some people finding support while others are dismissed by the family) impact thirteen-year-old Maya?

Excerpt #1:
Saturdays and Sundays are usually our busiest days—one, for the coffee, two, for a slammin' plate of huevos rancheros or panqueques. Café Taza is a family business in every sense of the word, so everybody has to pitch in—especially on weekends, especially during the summer. It's kind of a drag, and probably against some city's child labor laws, but we're all so used to it that there is no other way to live for us. Plus, who can afford summer camp? So whenever we aren't at school (or soccer practice for me), you can usually find three generations of Calderones at Café Taza in Fort Greene, Brooklyn, serving up mofongo, sandwiches de pernil, and—Brooklyn's best kept secret—the most epic cafés con leche in the borough. (pp. 2–3)

Excerpt #2:
One day, I asked Tio Fausto if Abuelo's grumblings are something to be worried about. My uncle says a lot of it is due to gentrification, which means the neighborhood is changing—and our main clientele is dwindling, because the new neighbors prefer the trendy restaurants over the local hangout spots. What used to be a working class Black and Latino neighborhood has morphed into mostly rich, white professionals, who buy up brownstones and storefronts and renovate them into something unrecognizable. As a result, the rents have gone up, driving families who have lived in Brooklyn for decades to find cheaper rent elsewhere. And prices for everything else have skyrocketed ... One thing about Puerto Ricans, though: We are a proud people who stay true to ourselves and do not give up—so the Calderones continue to center Café Taza around Mami's authentic criollo recipes. (pp. 12–13)

Excerpt #3
Abuela's side of the family is known as Los Locos—as Trini, who is always doling out the bochinche, tells us … there is the witch: Abuela's older sister, who still lives on the island. I don't know much about her, because she is estranged from the family and no one is supposed to mention her. All I've heard from Trini is that she is rumored to cast spells and sacrifice chickens and stuff. I don't like the idea that my great aunt, whom I've never met, is in Puerto Rico all by herself, while the rest of us are here in Brooklyn. It's almost as bad as Titi Dolores and my cousins being in California. We're supposed to be a tightknit family, and this vieja is all alone on an island. And also because, the truth is, sometimes I wonder if I am a little "loca" myself. Those dreams I have … sometimes they feel more real to me than serving up cafés con leche at Café Taza or dribbling the ball on the soccer pitch. And what scares me even more than the dreams is that I can never tell anyone in my family about them, ever. I can imagine the disappointed look on Abuela Chacha's face, the sound of Abuelo's scoffing, and Mami's concerned eyebrows. Being dismissed. And then, after that, the loneliness. (pp. 14–15)

WRITING

Without sharing further excerpts from the book, invite students to use their imagination, what they know from the three previous excerpts, and what they know about their lives to create a scene where the protagonist, Maya, confronts her family. Students can consider the following for their scene:

- Setting: Consider the importance of the Café Taza for the family.
- Characters: Maya is troubled by these vivid dreams that she has and by the way that her family views Titi Yaya.
- Dialogue: What would a thirteen-year-old say to a family member about these concerns? What would certain family members say? How would Abuela respond to Maya's "dreams" compared to how Titi Yaya would respond?

Place students in writing partnerships to brainstorm their (individual or partner) scene, draft, act out, and revise. These can be quick rehearsals of how a conversation might go. It's important for students to be allowed the room to explore these issues through a fictional character, as they can revisit later (within the same lesson or later lessons) the issue of how this looks in their lives. Sometimes, classroom teachers have partnered with school counselors or social workers to provide support on how youth can have difficult conversations with adults in their communities, especially when seeking healing or mutual understanding.

CLOSING DISCUSSION

Discuss mainstream media representations of minoritized faith communities like the one featured in *Salsa Magic*. What has been the reception of those representations? For example, when Brazilian artist Anitta released the music video "Aceita" (or "Accept"), which reveals her Candomblé faith, she lost 200,000 followers within the first two hours after the video was released (Mayorquín, 2024). According to Mayorquín's write-up of Anitta's "Aceita" music video reception,

> It wasn't until the 20th century that mainstream society began to tolerate expressions of Candomblé in an effort to recognize Brazil's African heritage and cultivate a stronger Brazilian national identity, said Luis Nicolau Parés … As acts of violence and discrimination targeting Candomblé and other Afro-Brazilian religions have persisted, activists have pointed to the issue of race … Anitta said she had been the subject of "religious racism," a term introduced by Candomblé leaders to describe acts of religious intolerance toward Afro-Brazilian faiths, Professor Lee said.
>
> (2024)

Invite students to discuss the following questions:

- What does it say when people critique faith traditions that come from minoritized Black and Indigenous populations but welcome those from white colonizers?
- How do those oppressed communities face this type of discrimination?
- What have been your reactions to recent news or social media conversations (i.e. artists, films, series, etc.) on this topic?
- How do these help you consider what you know about your local communities, spaces, and people who have shaped your family or loved ones' experiences?

Lesson #4: In the Heights: Communities That Elevate, Communities That Stifle: Young Adult Novel in Verse

The words in this chapter's opening quote from Melanie, "I wasn't really proud of who I was," serve to motivate us to find ways for our Latinx students to counter that push towards erasure, and to feel supported to find connections with others and the nurturing aspects of their ancestry. Educator Brendaly Torres in the last chapter's testimonio talked about the impact that author and poet Elisabet Velasquez had on her students, not only through the young adult novel in verse *When We Make It* (2021), but also through her school visit. Those are the pockets of hope, those moments of validation and chispa that I live for! That spark that will come when students see others like them, or others who have gone through similar experiences, and learn from their courage and love.

I've been connecting with Melanie for several semesters in her undergraduate studies, through my courses, emails, and texts, often sharing books, authors (especially those who, like her, are from Guatemala), and mentoring opportunities. I never want Melanie to feel like she has to hide parts of who she is in any educational setting. I know that, by the time this book is out in the world, I'll be preparing to celebrate Melanie at commencement, shouting her name from that stage. I write these words just hours after sharing in that special moment with my undergraduate students, all of whom read *When We Make It* with me for a book club. We shared our hope, our rage, our tears, and our connections. That book brought us together in ways I could've never imagined as a professor, and I'll forever be grateful to Elisabet Velasquez and Latine authors like her who help us feel seen and push us to think about the complexity of the Latinx diaspora.

WRITING LESSON #4

LESSON TEXTS

- "When We Make It: Meet Author Elisabet Velasquez" Penguin Teen video (2021)
- *When We Make It* by Elisabet Velasquez (2021)

OBJECTIVES

Discussion: Discuss the significance of a community in an author's writing and in our lives.

Text Analysis: Analyze how a character's relationship to a community reveals the parts of their identity that hold most significance.

Writing: Demonstrate how a poet's techniques inspire writing about a community in our lives through poetry.

OPENING DISCUSSION

Show students the video "When We Make It: Meet Author Elisabet Velasquez," available on the Penguin Teen YouTube channel (2021). Have students discuss why it was important for Elisabet to set her book in Bushwick, Brooklyn. Invite students to discuss comparisons with other texts where the setting was a significant character. Show students the book summary for *When We Make It* from the publisher's site before transitioning to the next part of the lesson.

TEXT ANALYSIS

Read the poems "Neighbors," "I Ask Questions About Puerto Rico," "The Neighborhood is Changing," and "Can I Be Puerto Rican?" as a class, and then assign groups to one poem for rereading and discussions. These are but a few of the many poems that address not just the specific community of Bushwick, Brooklyn, that we learned is so important to the author (and the protagonist in this novel in verse) but also the ways the protagonist's relationship to her own identity as a Puerto Rican in Brooklyn, New York, is shaped by her neighborhood. Invite students to ask:

- What are the characteristics of this community? How do they compare with my own?
- How do we know that this community is meaningful to the protagonist, Sarai? In other words, how does Elisabet reveal a sense of pride, wonderment, and authentic concern for her community through her character in these poems?
- How do these poems help us think about what shapes who we are and how we, in turn, have an impact on a place and other people?

Ask group participants to share with the class so others can learn about these poems and the group's analysis. Groups can begin by reading the poem and providing a summary of their conversation.

WRITING

Provide students with copies of all four poems so that they can select one as a guide for writing their own. Encourage students to try more than one, noticing which techniques they enjoy the most as writers!

- For example, those inspired by "Neighbors" can work on a poem about their neighborhood. Like Elisabet Velasquez, they can use their different senses to describe what they see, hear, taste, touch, and smell in their neighborhoods.
- For those inspired by "I Ask Questions About Puerto Rico," they can recall a time when they tried to have a conversation with an adult about a matter of importance to who they are but they were met with resistance. They might choose to borrow the first lines of the poem. Velasquez begins with "When I ask Mami to tell me about Puerto Rico / she says it's none of my business" (p. 18). The sentence frame could be: "When I ask _____ to tell me about _____, _____ says it's _____."
- The students who select "The Neighborhood is Changing" can consider a challenge that their community is facing and begin writing about a time when they witnessed this challenge, who was impacted, and how the community is responding.
- "Can I Be Puerto Rican?" is a great mentor-list poem for those students who've been doubted or received pushback when they've taken a stance expressing a part of their identity. Where is the doubt coming from? Why is it difficult to accept? Is there an internal doubt or turmoil that the student is grappling with because of societal pressures? What gets in the way of them being their full and authentic selves?

CLOSING DISCUSSION

When We Make It ends with a poem titled "What If Making It Looks Like This." Read the poem and ask students to identify their favorite "What if ..." and to explain why. How does this poem help them think about their own ideas and dreams for their community and for themselves (what does life after their time at this school look like?).

TESTIMONIO: Enrique Lopez Pino

Sixth-Grade English Language Arts and Eighth-Grade Social Studies Teacher, De La Salle Academy, New York City Independent School

I had the privilege of teaching Enrique when he was a graduate student in the Bilingual Teacher Preparation Program I taught at Hunter College, City University of New York. Since then, I've visited his middle-grade classroom and partnered Raúl Vaquero (testimonio in Chapter 3) with Enrique for a summer English program. This testimonio shows us Enrique's roots and evolution as an educator.

ENRIQUE ON HIS JOURNEY AS AN EDUCATOR:

I wasn't always certain I wanted to become a teacher. But I did know something that I did enjoy, and I did love just working with younger people but then I also quickly found out that I always tied it back to just my own story ... My family and I were undocumented for just about all of my childhood. I always tell of people that along the way, despite whatever financial or health hardships my family and I faced, we always had these educators who really cared for my family. Whether it was teachers that wanted to support us in our own immigration applications or wanted just to make sure that my family and I were doing well ...

I just always had teachers who either went out of their way to help me or my two older brothers. They saw this potential in us, and they definitely, you know, gave us every guidance. Especially as you know, first generation. We had no clue what we were doing. My parents had to work seven days a week every day without a day off, for, like, you know, twenty-plus years. So it was very confusing the whole process, especially as we got a little bit older ...

I've been fortunate to teach so many wonderful, first-generation families that are going through this process just like I did many years ago. I realized the fortune I had in my life, and I wanted to do the same and continue to give back to my community, give back to this younger generation of go-getters ...

My first year it was only [teaching] English Language Arts, and it was sixth, seventh, and eighth grade ELA. That was quite a year, definitely as a first-year teacher ... It was ups and downs. It was a lot of nights of stress. But a lot of nights of growth.

And I always told the administration that the craft I'm 100% dedicated to. I will focus, focus, focus, but the one thing I know for sure I can do now to the best of my ability is just that relationship-building with my students.

I think the first year was a process of getting to know what I wanted to do as an educator, but also as a process of learning from experts, learning from people who have done this for many years ...

That's been really, really helpful, as I've been trying to see what is it that I want to produce and grow in our own curriculum ... One of the first things I noticed is that we have one of the most diverse independent schools in the city, in the country, and our curriculum at that point, didn't reflect the stories of our students ... We revamped almost the entire reading curriculum from sixth grade. We've added a lot more like one of the things I've learned in my own journey is just providing greater choice in reading.

One of the things I was also proud of is this year I've started just to push myself to get my students outside of the classroom. One of the highlights of the year for me was when we studied the Great Migration and Harlem Renaissance. That was a totally new unit that I built off of reading excerpts from Isabel Wilkerson's work and showing them the Ted Talk. Then, by great fortune, the MET [Metropolitan Museum of Art] opened up their new exhibit, and I was able to take the whole eighth-grade class over there. Having them see those art pieces was beautiful.

ENRIQUE ON HIS FIRST MEMORY OF SEEING HIMSELF AS A WRITER:

On a personal level, as a writer, it took a bit. I think it was probably in High School, senior year. At that point in California they had different levels of writing like honors English, AP, etc. I never really put it together that by senior year, people were saying, *you're a really strong writer.* I didn't really, really reconnect that with myself.

ENRIQUE ON HIS FAVORITE WRITING ACTIVITY WITH LATINX TEENS:

There are two units I particularly love with sixth grade. One we're doing right now, which is the personal narrative unit, and then there's also the poetry unit. This poetry unit we started off with Elizabeth Acevedo's "Rat Ode" video on YouTube. She explains her own experiences with her professor who would say you can't write about a rat, like that's not an elegant enough animal ...

I remember this year we had a sixth grader who was really hesitant to do a little poetry and he was like, "I'm struggling with this." I said, "we're kind of going to talk, going over the process," and asked, "what is that first major hurdle we have here right?" And what we discovered was that up to that point he had always written poetry for somebody else. He was always trying to impress his teacher. I told him, "you know, this is you. This is for you. I'm gonna enjoy it. I'm gonna read it. I'm gonna love it right, no matter what it is. Right. But this is for your own self-discovery and self-growth." It was funny. The poem was about Minecraft actually, and his love for Minecraft. But once I told him that, he was really into it, and he wrote this beautiful poem all about seeing himself as that gamer, that love for his Minecraft there. But that was that step we had to get rid of "who am I writing for?"

ENRIQUE ON LATINX AUTHORS OR TEXTS GIVING HIM LIFE RIGHT NOW:

So there are three books we're going to add to the book club selections next year: *Merci Suárez Changes Gears*, a classic at this point. Also *Mexikid*. I was looking for a wonderful graphic novel ... and *Iveliz Explains It All*, I thought was going to connect. Also, just what we're all trying to do here is continue to build the multitude of experiences that we have as Latinx people.

ENRIQUE'S ADVICE FOR WRITING TEACHERS OF LATINX YOUTH:

I've gotten a little bit more comfortable with the idea of just taking risks with the curriculum and accepting that it's not always going to go smoothly. That's been really important for me to learn. The thought of a lesson not going super smoothly was really uncomfortable because I'd think, "I'm not a good educator or I'm not doing enough prep, or I'm not doing everything like what I'm supposed to be doing right." Now, I've embraced the idea that not every lesson is going to go super smoothly, or it's not going to connect ...

Also just gain a lot more student input, too. I think that's one thing that's changed from my first years, too, is being more comfortable with that student feedback ... I've had activities that I've taken years to develop, like this poetry unit that we just finished back in February.

ENRIQUE ON WRITING HE'S WORKING ON NOW:

I do reflection work or journal work. I do miss going back into more of the academic writing. I definitely miss my own ability to research but whatever activity I do with my students, I always tell them I'm sharing. I'll break the ice. I will share my work first. Whatever I'm asking you to do. I am also along with you, right? And I'm going to share my poetry and share my personal narrative.

Chapter Seven

Closing Reflection: We Can Be Many Things: Dispelling the Myth of the Latine Monolith

When I was conducting research on what would become *Escribiendo para desahogarme: Release and Resistance in a Middle School Bilingual Writing Workshop* (España, 2017), I knew my life would never be the same. Listening to Latine young people, reading their writing, watching their teacher share her writing, and processing these experiences with my mentor, Ofelia García, rocked me to my core. These middle-grade writers emboldened me to take my dreams and career goals in a different direction, including more interactions with Latinx youth and the educators in their lives. Maybe it was when one of the research participants, Genesis, encouraged newcomer students to write, saying "No te quedes callado porque te vas a sentir como más atascado y nunca vas a compartir eso. Te vas a sentir como ahogado" (España, 2017, p. 163). Perhaps it was also seeing their teacher

Posing with Mom in cueca attire in Chile

Dancing cueca in Queens, New York

Wearing cueca attire with Mom in New York

Dancing cueca in Queens, New York

create an environment open to their voices and experiences, rejecting traditional writing-workshop techniques and exhibiting what Felicia Rose Chavez (2021) advocates for in the must-read text for all writing instructors, *The Anti-Racist Writing Workshop: How to Decolonize the Creative Classroom.* These students' and their teacher's words have remained with me as I craft my writing experiences for school visits and college courses.

Writing with and for the young people in my life means I must remain open to learning more about these writers. I think back to Pre-K, elementary school, and eleventh-grade Carlita representing Chile at family and school Multicultural Day celebrations (pictured above), and I'm so grateful to the school staff who got to know me. Although I interacted with friends from all over the Latinx diaspora in my classes and at after-school activities, we had varied stories and interests.

The more I write with Latine youth, the more I'm reminded of those middle graders from my research and my friends from my high school. We are a varied bunch. Not all Latine youth: are immigrants; speak Spanish; are Christian; listen to and dance bachata, salsa, merengue, cumbia, and reggaeton; watch Mexican telenovelas; are from Mexico; or identify as Brown.

In one of my favorite pieces of writing, "Eres un Pocho," in the anthology *Wild Tongues Can't Be Tamed: Voices from the Latinx Diaspora*, *New York Times* bestselling author Mark Oshiro (2021) writes:

> You will simply tell your mother that there's nothing wrong with
> speaking another language,
> combing your hair a certain way,
> listening to music you love,
> being
> (brown)
> (queer)
> (your true self).
> You wish you could say those things aloud.
> You don't.
> Yet.
>
> (Oshiro, 2021, p. 8)

Oshiro writes from the perspective of a queer transracial Latinx adoptee, with these identities informing each other. Besides their craft (I'm also a fan of their young adult novel *Each One of Us a Desert*), I appreciate this approach to writing – writing your full self. Authors like Oshiro help us educators expand or complicate our ideas about Latinidad when teaching Latinx teen writers.

In "The Next Census Could Reveal a Very Different America" (Arroyo-Santiago, 2024), Nancy López and Alan Aja caution about the harmful decision by the United States Office of Management and Budget (OMB) to combine the race and ethnicity question and add Hispanic or Latino as a response option. They discuss how important it is to have data on income, employment, home values, and healthcare discrepancies when comparing Black Latinxs with other Latinxs. I appreciate that they start their piece by calling attention to the Mendez, et al. vs. Westminster (1947) U.S. Supreme Court decision (United States Courts, n.d.), one that several of my students read of in Duncan Tonatiuh's picture book, *Separate is Never Equal: Sylvia Mendez and Her Family's Fight for Desegregation* (2014). Sylvia, a Mexican Puerto Rican child, was not allowed to enroll in her neighborhood school in California with her family members because she was of darker skin (compared to her lighter-skinned cousins who were allowed enrollment). Not many people know about Sylvia Mendez and this court case, but I like to remind my students often because not only is it recent history, but it is a reminder that many of us have different experiences, even within our Latinx community.

Recently, I had the opportunity to visit a school in El Paso, Texas, thanks to an invitation from Professor Dan Heiman at the University of Texas at El Paso (UTEP). My conversations with the shuttle driver, hotel staff, UTEP students, and faculty all featured characteristics specific to migration in that area, especially for those living across the United States-Mexico border and studying at UTEP or working in El Paso. This was a very different experience from that of the Latinx students at Kennesaw State University in Georgia you read about in the previous chapter's narrative.

My current students, most of them future teachers in New York City Public Schools, tell of the ways their school sites (for fieldwork and student teaching) are creating new classes and programs for newcomer students arriving from Venezuela, Haiti, and Central America. Some of my students talk about how gentrification is impacting their neighborhoods and how Latinx students in bilingual dual language programs are not benefitting from the original intention of the programming. Nelson Flores and Ofelia García (2017) talk about this complexity and inequity in bilingual programs with the Latinx community, stating the following:

> To be clear, we both believe that bilingual education continues to offer the possibility of challenging the marginalization of Latinx and other minoritized students. Yet, as we reflect on the history of the field in the post–Civil Rights era, we lament the fact that the lofty goals of original proponents of these programs within the Latinx

> community have not been fully achieved. The failure of bilingual education to meet these lofty goals should not be interpreted as a failure of bilingual education, but rather as a failure of U.S. society to address the underlying racialization processes that relegate Latinx and other minoritized communities to second-class status in U.S. society.
>
> (p. 16)

Flores and García (2017) push our thinking as we must consider the intent of our programming that is supposed to serve Latinx communities and their reality. This concern also applies to emergent bilinguals labeled as disabled (EBLADs) and their families, as scholar María Cioè-Peña (2021) writes in her award-winning book *(M)othering Labeled Children: Bilingualism and Disability in the Lives of Latinx Mothers*.

Representing all Latine youth experiences in one book is impossible because our community is vast and varied. I started chapters with words from Latine students from my research and ended with testimonios of Latine educators in my life, hoping to give you a glimpse of this complexity. Sixth graders Oscary, Genesis, and Ana and undergraduate students Jenifer, Sara, Paola, and Melanie had different experiences writing in school and feeling accepted in that community. Educators Anel V. Rivera Guerrero, Raúl Vaquero, Coral Zayas, Brendaly Torres, and Enrique Lopez Pino are all in New York State. Yet their roles and communities require deep listening to their particular Latinx students. I've been reflecting on and expressing to them how their expertise connects so well with this student population. Anel advocates for the EBLADs and newcomers in her context, while Raúl and Enrique redesign the curriculum for representation and criticality. Coral and Brendaly bring the administrator lens to their work with multiple teachers and students, considering culturally and linguistically sustaining (Paris & Alim, 2017) curriculum design and professional development sessions. They're all writers in their own way as well, and cultivating that identity as Latinx educators is necessary in their work with youth and adults.

This is the first book where I share my creative writing in a text for educators, and I hope it has moved you to nurture your own writing. Whether you are working on morning pages like Raúl, programming and policy documents like Coral, or curriculum like Anel, Enrique, and Brendaly, you can forge that path in community. Although I am in different writing groups across the year and write steadily with my hermana en la lucha, Luz Yadira Herrera, I've been growing so much as a creative writer with the works of poets Ariana Brown and Elisabet Velasquez, who give helpful writing life recommendations on social media.

There's so much more to us and our writing identity, which is why I chose to share my go-to poets, authors, and films for these conversations on writing with Latinx youth. Although the topics featured in this book don't encompass all of our experiences (migration, mental health, language, resilience, and communities), the texts I shared do cut across these and other topics. The teacher text sets and student text sets are also there to serve as entry points into this work as Latinx authors, poets, scholars, public intellectuals, journalists, and artists continue to give us much to process. These curated lists should be interactive and can live inside the writers' classroom and beyond it. Even though books with at least one Latine creator (author, illustrator, or compiler) only made up 11% of the children's and young adult books in 2023 (based on the 3,491 books received from publishers by the Cooperative Children's Book Center, CCBC [2024]), I remain hopeful because of the writers I featured in this book, including the middle-grade and undergraduate students from my research!

Alan Pelaez Lopez (2023) in the introduction to their beautifully edited anthology, *When Language Broke Open: An Anthology of Queer and Trans Black Writers of Latin American Descent*, writes, "In claiming back our narratives, memories, experiences, and imaginations, we defend our right to speak" (p. xxii). As an Afro-Indigenous (Zapotec) poet, and installation and adornment artist from Oaxaca, Mexico, Pelaez Lopez uses art as mourning and civil disobedience. Their "Latinidad is Cancelled" (2018) social practice project seeks to encourage us all to imagine futures "where all people of Latin America and its diasporas are no longer forced into a single-dimensional narrative" (Pelaez Lopez, n.d.). I am grateful for their work that is pushing my own thinking on what it means to support our Latine youth's imaginations and memory.

May the words of the brave, curious, and critical youth and creators of Latin American descent featured in this book reverberate in your writing communities. May their testimonios ground you and guide you in growing creative ways to combat censorship, bans, and decontextualized scripted curricula. I leave with you *Narrative Writing with Latinx Teens: Testimonios, Texts, and Teaching* as one of many ways we can connect, and hope that our paths cross so we can commune, write, and heal together.

Appendix A
Testimonio Questions

1. Tell me about your journey as an educator. What did you start teaching, and what is your role now? How have you evolved as an educator through these roles?
2. What is your first memory when you saw yourself as a writer or writing teacher?
3. What is your favorite writing lesson, activity, or prompt to use with Latinx teens? Why?
4. Can you tell us a little about a Latinx author or book giving you life right now?
5. What is one piece of advice you would give writing teachers of Latinx teens, something you'd wish you would've known early on in your writing with young people?
6. Bonus: What are you working on in your writing right now, and who are your writing mentors for this piece?

Appendix B

Poetry as Teaching, Resistance, and Healing Framework

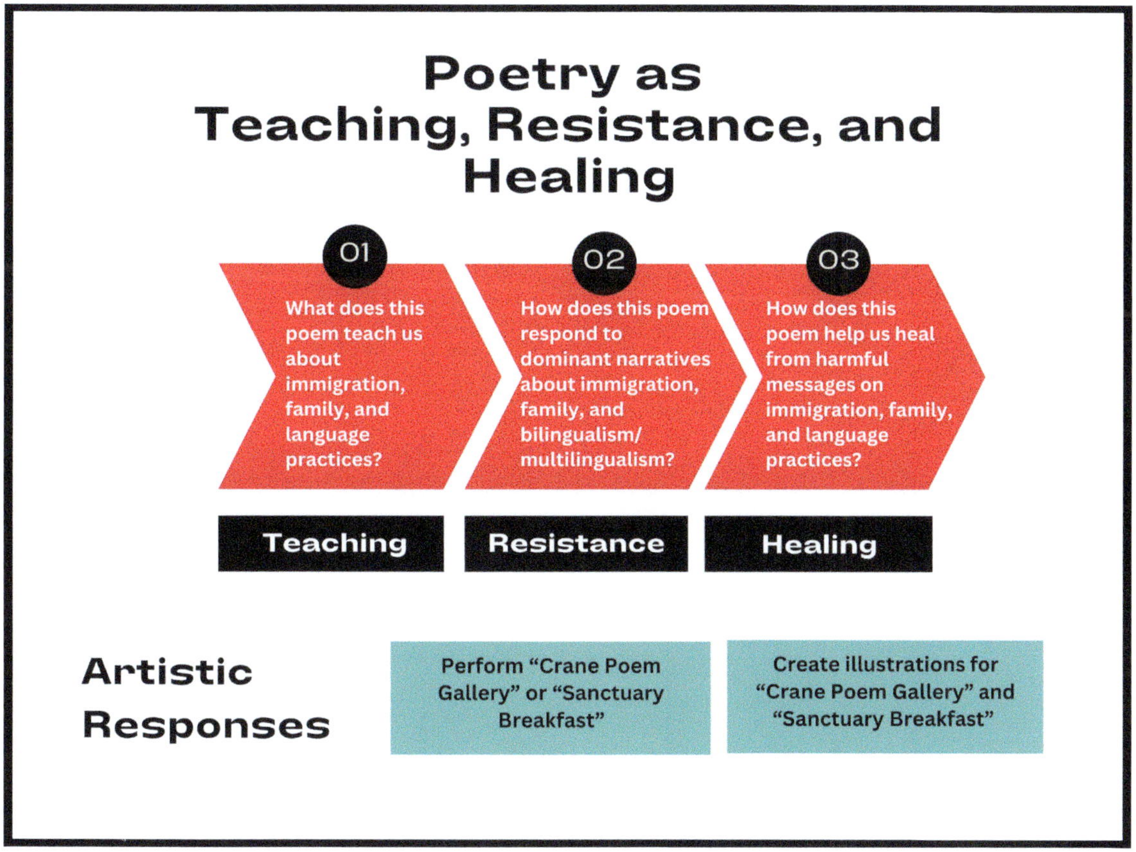

Appendix C
Amplifying Counter-narratives

AMPLIFYING COUNTERNARRATIVES

Dominant Narrative	Counter Narrative	Bilingual or Multilingual Definition
What words are most associated with this topic?	What words are missing from the popular narrative on this topic?	What would a definition on this topic sound like if we centered the counter narrative?
What images and sounds are the ones that get shared the most on this topic?	What images and sounds should be made more popular on this topic?	What might it look like if we considered different languages?
Who are the loudest voices on this topic?	Who are the voices that are silenced or ignored on this topic?	

Adapted from *En Comunidad: Lessons for Centering the Voices and Experiences of Bilingual Latinx Students* by Carla España and Luz Yadira Herrera (Fig. 4.6 on page 91)

Appendix D

Types of Writing Lessons

Lessons	Chapter 2	Chapter 3	Chapter 4	Chapter 5	Chapter 6
Multimodal	**Documentary Reflection** "In the past, when I thought of/saw/heard ____, I used to immediately associate it with ____. I realized I needed to learn more when I …"	Use primary sources to create an **action plan** to support students' well-being at school.	Compose a **short narrative** that can be used as a case study/simulation scenario for teachers, administrators, and language policymakers to learn about translanguaging.	Develop an **annotated outline for a TED Talk** to share ideas on expectations, perceptions, and their impact on our lives.	Write a **script** that follows an opening musical scene in a film.
Poetry	Use the prompt, "I was ____ years old when I first ____" to write a **poem**.	Write a **poem** using the "borrowing a line" strategy inspired by "Sanctuary" or "After the Fire" by Ada Limón.	Try different poetry brainstorming prompts and strategies to write a "Translation for ____" **poem**.	Create a **poem** that extends a metaphor in response to Yesenia Montilla's "a brief meditation on breath."	Select from two different poetry structures to write a **poem** about a community.
MG	Build off of writing partner/group discussions to write **poems** about an object that reveals a connection with someone meaningful to the writer.	Create a **fictional character, problem, and feeling to set up a story** using Andrea Beatriz Arango's recommended poetic devices (rhyme, repetition, varying sentence length).	Demonstrate how to use different genres (realistic fiction, historical fiction, speculative fiction) to develop a **scene** focused on a protagonist and how they approach their life challenges.	Create a **scene** that reveals how a character deals with the tension of trying to be themselves and live joyfully while facing different expectations from loved ones.	Create a **fan-fiction scene** that builds on what we know about a character's motivations and challenges from the text's first chapter.
YA	Develop a scene that shows what we know about the impact of immigration policies and the characteristics of **speculative fiction**.	Consider different writing formats (journal entry, meditation, community norms) to expand on deep feelings.	Develop **interview questions** for writing partnerships to review and share information on Indigenous languages in Mexico.	Brainstorm **visual representations** of a character's words and actions and their impact on your life.	Demonstrate how a poet's techniques inspire writing about a community in our lives through **poetry**.

Appendix E
Mentor Texts and Media

<table>
<tr><th colspan="4">Chapter 2: "Soy de aquí y de allá": Migration, Immigration, and Moves That Upend Lives</th></tr>
<tr><td colspan="4">Teacher Sample Writing
■ Poem: "Remember Me"
■ Personal narrative: "The Layover"</td></tr>
<tr><th>Lesson #1</th><th>Lesson #2</th><th>Lesson #3</th><th>Lesson #4</th></tr>
<tr>
<td>We Still Here documentary trailer
Investigative journalist Bianca Graulau's documentary Aquí Vive Gente on Bad Bunny's "El Apagón" music video [begins at 4:35 minutes].
Sí, Se Puede: The Latino Heroes who Changed the United States graphic novel by Julio Anta, illustrated by Yasmín Flores Montañez</td>
<td>Ariana Brown's "23" spoken word poetry performance
Conversation: "Afro-Mexican Poetics" conversation and poetry readings with Alan Pelaez Lopez and Ariana Brown
Darrel Alejandro Holnes' "Amending Wall" poem on the Poetry Unbound podcast</td>
<td>"Crane Poem Gallery" and "Sanctuary Breakfast" by Aida Salazar in Land of the Cranes
Imagine by Juan Felipe Herrera (poem, picture book, or video)
Hear My Voice/ Escucha mi voz: The Testimonies of Children Detained at the Southern Border of the United States (book trailer)</td>
<td>The Grief Keeper by Alexandra Villasante
Latinx KidLit Book Festival "Fantastical y Más Fuerte: Contemporary Takes on Immigration" video</td>
</tr>
</table>

Chapter 3: Estamos bien: Talking Mental Health and Breaking Stigmas			
Teacher Sample Writing ■ Poem: "Lost on Queens Boulevard" ■ Personal narrative: "Para ser bella, hay que ver estrellas"			
Lesson #1	**Lesson #2**	**Lesson #3**	**Lesson #4**
"The Kids Are Not Alright: The Mental Health Crisis Affecting Latina Teens" Vice video. GLSEN National School Climate Survey and State Snapshot	*The Carrying* and *The Hurting Kind* by Ada Limón "To Be Made Whole" *On Being* podcast episode (features poems from *The Carrying* and *The Hurting Kind*) *The Pain We Carry: Healing from Complex PTSD for People of Color* by Natalie Y. Gutiérrez	*Iveliz Explains It All* by Andrea Beatriz Arango *The Horn Book Magazine* "Publishers' Preview: Debut Authors: Five Questions for Andrea Beatriz Arango" Latinx KidLit Book Festival "How Do Writers Use Poetry to Tell a Story with Andrea Beatriz Arango" video Follet Learning "First Chapter Friday: *Iveliz Explains It All* by Andrea Beatriz Arango" video	*The Making of Yolanda La Bruja* by Lorraine Avila "Lorraine Avila Talks Being an Author and Using Her Voice to Stand Up for Issues in Her Community" *Growing Up Latina* podcast episode video "Lorraine Avila's Debut Novel Explores Brujería, Afro-Latina Girlhood, and Community" by Sofia Aguilar for *Hip Latina* website

Chapter 4: Learning a New Language, Learning a New Me			
Teacher Sample Writing ■ Poem: "ESL" ■ Narrative: "Saturday School: La Escuela Argentina"			
Lesson #1	**Lesson #2**	**Lesson #3**	**Lesson #4**
"Translanguaging in 15 Minutes" by Dr. Mike Mena on *The Social Life of Language* YouTube channel	"Translation" by Yesika Salgado (spoken word performance) "Translation for Mamá" and "My Father in English" poems by Richard Blanco in *Homeland of My Body: New and Selected Poems*	***The Year I Flew Away*** by Marie Arnold *We Need Diverse Books* blog "Marie Arnold Writes So Immigrant Readers Feel Seen" by Karis Rogerson	"Karla Sánchez and Yásnaya Elena Aguilar Gil" from *Daughters of Latin America: An International Anthology of Writing by Latine Women* edited by Sandra Guzmán

<table>
<tr><th colspan="4">Chapter 5: Vamos a resolver y florecer: Resourcefulness, Resilience, and Recovery</th></tr>
<tr><td colspan="4">Teacher Sample Writing
■ Poem: "Ponte las pilas ... is Canceled"
■ Personal narrative: "Self-Portrait with Cropped Hair"</td></tr>
<tr><th>Lesson #1</th><th>Lesson #2</th><th>Lesson #3</th><th>Lesson #4</th></tr>
<tr><td>America Ferrera's monologue in the Barbie film
America Ferrera's TED Talk, "My Identity is a Superpower"</td><td>"Yesenia Montilla: Poet Profile" by Jasminne Mendez
"a brief meditation on breath" by Yesenia Montilla</td><td>Frizzy by Claribel Ortega</td><td>"American Street: The American Dream and the Immigrant Imagination," Ibi Zoboi presentation at Vanderbilt University
American Street by Ibi Zoboi</td></tr>
</table>

<table>
<tr><th colspan="4">Chapter 6: In the Heights: Communities That Elevate, Communities That Stifle</th></tr>
<tr><td colspan="4">Teacher Sample Writing
■ Poem: "I Was Told to Leave 'All that Multicultural Work' for My 'Urban' Schools"
■ Personal narrative: "Latinx Teacher Retreat"</td></tr>
<tr><th>Lesson #1</th><th>Lesson #2</th><th>Lesson #3</th><th>Lesson #4</th></tr>
<tr><td>In the Heights film opening scene
In the Heights interviews with writer and producer Quiara Alegría Hudes and actors Leslie Grace and Gregory Diaz IV</td><td>"No existe un mundo poshuracán: Puerto Rican Art in the Wake of Hurricane María" Whitney Museum of American Art YouTube video
"the independence (of puerto rico)" / "la independencia (de puerto rico)" by Roque Raquel Salas Rivera
"Chicago Poet José Olivarez: Straddling Two Cultures and How It's Impacted His Art" on La Vida Baseball YouTube channel
"No Time to Wait" by José Olivarez</td><td>"Interview with Author Letisha Marrero" on the Women of Color Read, Too blog
Salsa Magic by Letisha Marrero
Dominican Writers Association "Letisha Marrero Brings Us on a Spiritual Journey in Salsa Magic"</td><td>"When We Make It: Meet Author Elisabet Velasquez" Penguin Teens video
When We Make It by Elisabet Velasquez</td></tr>
</table>

References

Acevedo, E. (2018). *The poet x*. HarperCollins.

Aguilar, S. (2023, May 26). Lorraine Avila's debut novel explores brujería, Afro-Latina girlhood, and community. *Hip Latina*. www.hiplatina.com/lorraine-avila-yolanda-la-bruja

All Def Poetry (2015, July 15). Yesika Salgado - "Translation" - all def poetry x da poetry lounge [Video]. YouTube. www.youtube.com/watch?v=P5NSNwDB_08

Anta, J. (2023). *Sí se puede: The Latino heroes who changed the United States* (Y. Flores Montañez, Illus.). Ten Speed Graphic.

Anzaldúa, G. (1987). *Borderlands/ la frontera: The new mestiza* (1st ed.). Spinsters/ Aunt Lute.

Arango, B. (2022). *Iveliz explains it all*. Penguin Random House.

Arnold, M. (2021). *The year I flew away*. HarperCollins.

Arroyo-Santiago, C. (2024, May 3). Opinion: The next census could reveal a very different America. CNN. www.cnn.com/2024/04/30/opinions/census-race-ethnicity-omb-standards-arroyo-santiago/index.html

Avila, L. (2023). *The making of Yolanda la bruja*. Levine Querido.

Bad Bunny (2022, September 16). Bad Bunny - El Apagón - Aquí Vive Gente (Official Video) - Un Verano Sin Ti [Video]. YouTube. www.youtube.com/watch?v=1TCX_Aqzoo4

Balcárcel, R. (2019). *The other half of happy*. Chronicle Books.

Balcárcel, R. [SixMinuteScholar] (n.d.). SixMinuteScholar. www.youtube.com/channel/UCgDFMTONQz-JLXj3nM6MpiQ

Bean, B. (2020). Raciolinguistic ideologies and decolonizing anthropology: A conversation with Jonathan Rosa. AnthroPod, *Fieldsights*, February 24. www.culanth.org/fieldsights/raciolinguistic-ideologies-and-decolonizing-anthropology-a-conversation-with-jonathan-rosa

Blanco, R. (2023). *Homeland of my body: New and selected poems*. Penguin Random House.

Brooklyn College City University of New York Office of the Associate Provost for Institutional Effectiveness (n.d.). *Brooklyn College Fast Facts 2023–2024.* www.brooklyn.edu/wp-content/uploads/PROVOST-IE-Brooklyn-College-Factsheet.pdf

Bush, J. (Director, Writer), Howard, B. (Director, Writer), Castro Smith, C. (Director, Writer), Lee, J. (Producer), Merino, Y. (Producer), & Spencer, C. (Producer) (2021). *Encanto* [Film]. Walt Disney Animation Studies.

Button Poetry. [Button Poetry] (2018, July 30). Ariana Brown - "23" [Video]. YouTube. www.youtube.com/watch?v=RYMDA--KPqQ

Button Poetry. [Button Poetry] (2018, August 2). Jonathan Mendoza - "Confessions on gratitude" [Video]. YouTube. www.youtube.com/watch?v=MUHHVKU_L9A&t=2s

Castillo, A. (2023, September 19). *Letisha Marrero brings us on a spiritual journey in "Salsa Magic."* Dominican Writers Association. www.dominicanwriters.com/amp/letisha-marrero-brings-us-on-a-spiritual-journey-in-salsa-magic

Center for Disease Control (CDC) (2021). United States, High School Youth Risk Behavior Survey, 2021. https://nccd.cdc.gov/youthonline/App/Default.aspx

Chavez, F.R. (2021). *The anti-racist writing workshop: How to decolonize the creative classroom.* Haymarket Books.

Cherry-Paul, Sonja (2024). *Antiracist reading revolution (grades K-8): A framework for teaching beyond representation toward liberation.* Corwin.

Chu, J.M. (Director), Hudes, Q.A. (Producer, Writer), Miranda, L.M. (Producer, Writer), Bregman, A. (Producer), Jacobs, M. (Producer), & Sanders, S. (Producer) (2021). *In the Heights* [Film]. Warner Bros.

Cioè-Peña, M. (2020). Raciolinguistics and the education of emergent bilinguals labeled as disabled. *Urban Review, 53*, 443–469. https://doi.org/10.1007/s11256-020-00581-z

Cioè-Peña, M. (2021). *(M)othering labeled children: Bilingualism and disability in the lives of Latinx mothers.* Multilingual Matters.

Cisneros, D. (1984). *The house on Mango Street.* Arte Público Press.

Cooperative Children's Book Center, University of Wisconsin-Madison School of Education (2024, April 3). CCBC's Diversity Statistics show small changes in number of diverse books for children and teens published last year [Press release]. https://uwmadison.app.box.com/s/rn4ccrdx8f8a2nbbqb6spx16kxcy52r1/file/1490478755959

CUNY-NYSIEB (2019). Our teacher leaders. www.cuny-nysieb.org/classroom-videos/ambassador

Danticat, E. (2022). *Behind the mountains.* Scholastic (original work published 2002).

de los Ríos, C.V., & Seltzer, K. (2017). Translanguaging, coloniality, and English classrooms: An exploration of two bicoastal urban classrooms. *Research in the Teaching of English, 52*(1), 55–76. https://doi.org/10.58680/rte201729200

España, C. (2017). Escribiendo para desahogarme: Release and resistance in a middle school bilingual writing workshop (Publication No. 2119) [Doctoral dissertation, CUNY Graduate Center]. *CUNY Academic Works.* www.academicworks.cuny.edu/gc_etds/2119

España, C. & Herrera, L.Y. (2020). *En comunidad: Lessons for centering the voices and experiences of bilingual Latinx students.* Heinemann.

España, C., Herrera, L.Y., & Sánchez Hernández, M. (forthcoming). Exploring the impact of Latinx children's literature on bilingual teacher preparation: A study of Beauty Woke and Le dicen fregona. *International Journal of Critical Pedagogy* - Special Issue: Centering Love, Tension and Agency in Teacher Education.

Ethyle R. Wolfe Institute. [The Ethyle R. Wolfe Institute for the Humanities] (2024, May 8). Tony Kushner: Writing for My life [Video]. YouTube. www.youtube.com/live/5u6Tkbs_2c4?feature=shared

Faulstich Orellana, M. (2009). *Translating childhoods: Immigrant youth, language, and culture.* Rutgers University Press.

Faulstich Orellana, M. (n.d.). *Language brokering.* Marjorie Faulstich Orellana. www.marjoriefaulstichorellana.com/archive/language-brokering

Flores, N. (2020). From academic language to language architecture: Challenging raciolinguistic ideologies in research and practice. *Theory Into Practice, 59*(1), 22–31.

Flores, N., & García, O. (2017). A critical review of bilingual education in the United States: From basements and pride to boutiques and profit. *Annual Review of Applied Linguistics, 37*, 14–29. https://doi.org/10.1017/S0267190517000162

Flores, N., & Rosa, J. (2015). Undoing appropriateness: Raciolinguistic ideologies and language diversity in education. *Harvard Educational Review, 85*(2), 149–171.

Follet Learning (2022, August 15). First chapter Friday: *Iveliz explains it all* by Andrea Beatriz Arango [Video]. YouTube. www.youtube.com/watch?v=Ual4lM0o0B8

Freire, P. (1970). *Pedagogy of the oppressed.* Continuum.

García, O. (2009). *Bilingual education in the 21st century: A global perspective.* Wiley/Blackwell.

García, O. (2012). Theorizing translanguaging for educators. In C. Celic & K. Seltzer (Eds.), *Translanguaging: A CUNY-NYSIEB guide for educators.* CUNY-NYSIEB, The Graduate Center, The City University of New York. www.cuny-nysieb.org/wp-content/uploads/2016/04/Translanguaging-Guide-March-2013.pdf

García, O., & Leiva, C. (2014). Theorizing and enacting translanguaging for social justice. In A. Creese & A. Blackledge (Eds.), *Heteroglossia as practice and pedagogy* (pp. 199–216). Springer.

García, O. (2015). Language. In *The Wiley Blackwell Encyclopedia of Race, Ethnicity, and Nationalism* at Wiley Online Library. John Wiley & Sons, Ltd. Retrieved from www.onlinelibrary.wiley.com.central.ezproxy.cuny.edu:2048/doi/10.1002/97811186632

García, O., & Kleyn, T. (Eds.) (2016). *Translanguaging with multilingual students: Learning from classroom moments.* New York: Routledge.

García, O., Ibarra Johnson, S., & Seltzer, K. (2017). *The translanguaging classroom: Leveraging student bilingualism for learning.* Caslon.

García, O., Flores, N., Seltzer, K., Wei, L., Otheguy, R., & Rosa, J. (2021). Rejecting abyssal thinking in the language and education of racialized bilinguals: A manifesto. *Critical Inquiry in Language Studies, 18*(3), 203–228. https://doi.org/10.1080/15427587.2021.1935957

Gates Jr., H.L. (Producer, Writer) (2011). *Black in Latin America* [Series]. PBS.

GLSEN (n.d.). School climate survey. www.glsen.org/school-climate-survey

González, A.R. (2020). Reclaiming ourselves: Healing toward gender autonomy in our classrooms. In S.W. Woolley & L. Airton (Eds.), *Teaching about gender diversity: Teacher-tested lesson plans for K-12 classrooms* (pp. 169–177). Canadian Scholars.

González, A. R. (2023). The burden of acting human: Rethinking race, class, and gender experiences in U.S. independent schools. *Teachers College Record,* 125(7-8), 52–76. https://doi.org/10.1177/01614681231194406

González Martínez, E. (2021, March 9). Will the media get past the "resiliency" of Puerto Ricans? *Women's Media Center IDAR/E.* www.womensmediacenter.com/idare/the-media-leans-on-how-puerto-ricans-grin-and-bear-crisis

Gutiérrez, N.Y. (2022). *The pain we carry: Healing from complex PTSD for people of color.* New Harbinger.

Guzmán, S. (Ed.) (2023). *Daughters of Latin America: An international anthology of writing by Latine women.* HarperCollins.

Hernández Linares, L., & Rise Home Stories Project (2021). *Alejandria fights back!/ ¡La lucha de Alejandria!* (R.L. Trujillo, Illus.). Feminist Press.

Herrera, J.F. (2020). *Social distancing.* Poets.org. www.poets.org/poem/social-distancing

Herrera, J.F. (2021). *Imagine.* Candelwick Press.

Hinojosa, M. (Host) (2023, December 15). Still hopeful: Immigration over 30 years [Audio podcast episode]. In *Latino USA.* National Public Radio. www.latinousa.org/2023/12/15/immigration30years/

Huber, L., & Villanueva, B. (2019). Testimonio. In P. Atkinson, S. Delamont, A. Cernat, J.W. Sakshaug, & R.A. Williams (Eds.), SAGE Research Methods Foundations. https://doi.org/10.4135/9781526421036782944

Imarisha, W., Brown, A.M., & Thomas, S.R. (2015). *Octavia's brood: Science fiction stories from social justice movements*. AK Press.

Isasi-Díaz, A.M. (2001). *Participation in the divine: With God on a picket line*. The Way Supplement. www.theway.org.uk/back/s100Isasi-Diaz.pdf

Jacobs-Fantauzzi, E. (Director), Castillo Muñoz, A. (Writer), & Ortiz, M. (Writer) (2022). *We still here* [Film]. Clenched Fist Productions.

Jones, M. (2021, June 15). *In the Heights* writer Quiara Alegría Hudes "didn't want it to come off like a corny musical." *Entertainment Weekly*. www.ew.com/movies/in-the-heights-writer-quiara-alegria-hudes

Jorgensen, J. (2024, January 3). Migrant families to begin moving next week as 60-day shelter deadline nears. *Spectrum News NY 1*. www.ny1.com/nyc/all-boroughs/education/2024/01/03/migrant-families-to-begin-moving-next-week-as-60-day-shelter-deadline-nears

Joseph, L. (2001). *The color of my words*. HarperCollins.

Latinx KidLit Book Festival (2020, December 3). *Fantastical y más fuerte: Contemporary takes on immigration* [Video]. YouTube. www.youtube.com/watch?v=Yp7kq_COVCA

Latinx KidLit Book Festival (2022, September 12). How do writers use poetry to tell a story? with Andrea Beatriz Arango [Video]. YouTube. www.youtube.com/watch?v=OjxvCkUeyug

Latinx KidLit Book Festival (2023, September 29). Frizzy book club [Video]. YouTube. www.youtube.com/watch?v=-wYuC2WIUSU

La Vida Baseball (2019, September 10). Chicago Poet José Olivarez: Straddling two cultures and how it's impacted his art [Video]. YouTube. www.youtube.com/watch?v=CpwZwrIdYXU

Limón, A. (2021). *The carrying*. Milkweed Editions.

Limón, A. (2022). *The hurting kind*. Milkweed Editions.

Limón, A. (2023, July 23). Sanctuary - Written and read by Ada Limón. [Video]. The On Being project. YouTube. www.youtube.com/watch?v=Uz_QVPYHUR0

Lorde, A. (1988). *A burst of light and other essays.* Dover.

Marrero, L. (2023). *Salsa magic.* Levine Querido.

Max. (2023, December 22). America Ferrera's iconic Barbie speech [Video]. YouTube. www.youtube.com/watch?v=CBqlDWHkdHk

Mayorquín, O. (2024, March 18). Backlash to Anitta's music video evokes a painful history in Brazil. *The New York Times.* www.nytimes.com/2024/05/18/arts/anitta-brazil-candomble.html

Mendez, J. (2018, November 1). Yesenia Montilla. *Jasminne Mendez Blog.* www.jasminnemendez.com/blog?category=Poet%20Profiles.

Mendoza, J. (2019). Lines of work: Five poets on their day jobs. *Poetry Foundation.* www.poetryfoundation.org/articles/151079/lines-of-work

Montilla, Y. (2020). *A brief meditation on breath.* Academy of American Poets. www.poets.org/poem/brief-meditation-breath

Moraga, C.L. (2011). *A Xicana codex of changing consciousness: Writings 2000–2010.* Duke University Press.

Ms. WOC Reads (2024, March 13). Interview with Author Letisha Marrero. Women of Color Read, Too. www.womenofcolorreadtoo.blogspot.com/2024/03/interview-with-author-letisha-marrero.html

National Center for Education Statistics (2023). English Learners in Public Schools. *Condition of Education.* U.S. Department of Education, Institute of Education. www.nces.ed.gov/programs/coe/indicator/cgf

National Council of Teachers of English (2016). *What anti-racist language teachers do.* Standing Committee Against Racism and Bias in the Teaching of English. NCTE. https://ncte.org/app/uploads/2018/07/WhatAntiRacistLanguageTeachersDo.pdf

National Education Association (2020). English language learners: Toolkit. Retrieved [March 4, 2024], from www.nea.org/resource-library/english-language-learners

Nieman Foundation for Journalism at Harvard (2016, September 10). Nieman Curator Ann Marie Lipinski's conversation with Lin-Manuel Miranda at Pulitzer Centennial [Video]. YouTube. www.youtube.com/watch?v=LR6H77dM5F0&t=1s

Nieto, S. (2015). *Brooklyn dreams: My life in public education*. Harvard Education Press.

Nye, N.S. (2008). Gate A-4. Retrieved from www.poets.org/poem/gate-4

Olivarez, J. (2023). *Promises of gold/ Promesas de oro*. Macmillan.

Ortega, C.A. (2022). *Frizzy* (R. Bousamra, Illus.). Macmillan.

Ó Tuama, P. (Host) (2021, November 15). Darrel Alejandro Holnes: Amending Wall [Audio podcast episode]. In *Poetry unbound*. The On Being Project. www.onbeing.org/programs/darrel-alejandro-holnes-amending-wall

Ó Tuama, P. (Host) (2023, May 26). José Olivarez: No Time to Wait [Audio podcast episode]. In *Poetry unbound*. The On Being Project. https://www.onbeing.org/programs/jose-olivarez-no-time-to-wait

Oshiro, M. (2020). *Each of us a desert*. Macmillan.

Oshiro, M. (2021). Eres un pocho. In S.J. Fennell (Ed.), *Wild tongues can't be tamed: 15 voices from the Latinx diaspora* (p. 8). Macmillan.

Otheguy, R., Garcia, O., & Reid, W. (2015). Clarifying translanguaging and deconstructing named languages: A perspective from linguistics. *Applied Linguistics Review*, 6(3), 281–307.

Paris, D., & Alim, H.S. (Eds.) (2017). *Culturally sustaining pedagogies: Teaching and learning for justice in a changing world*. Teachers College Press.

Parra, J. (2022). *Growing an artist: The story of a landscaper and his son* (J. Parra, Illus.). Simon & Schuster.

PBS News Hour (2021, June 11). Watch: Leslie Grace on how "In the Heights" brings crucial Latinx stories to the screen [Video]. YouTube. www.youtube.com/watch?v=emINuiU7e7c

Pelaez Lopez, A. [Alan C. Pelaez Lopez] (2020, April 15). Afro-Mexican poetics [Video]. YouTube. www.youtube.com/watch?v=zvLpBHU5lQs

Pelaez Lopez, A. (2023). *When language broke open: An anthology of queer and trans Black writers of Latin American descent*. The University of Arizona Press.

Pelaez Lopez, A. (n.d.). Alan Pelaez Lopez: About. www.alanpelaez.com/about-me

Penguin Teen (2021, September 21). When we make it: Meet Elisabet Velasquez [Video]. YouTube. www.youtube.com/watch?v=79ljIhK5xhs

Pérez y González, M.E. (2021). How a few students transformed the ivory tower: Puerto Rican Studies and its (r)evolution at Brooklyn College. In M.E. Pérez y González & V. Sánchez Korrol (Eds.), *Puerto Rican studies in the City University of New York: The first 50 years*. Centro Press.

Portland State University (1975, May 30). Black Studies Center Public Dialogue, Part 2: Toni Morrison, Primus St. John, John Callahan, Susan Callahan, Lloyd Baker. *Special Collections: Oregon Public Speakers*. 90. www.pdxscholar.library.pdx.edu/orspeakers/90

Professional Staff Congress, City University of New York (2024, May 1). Arrests at City College: Statement from the PSC Principal Officers. www.psc-cuny.org/news-events/arrests-at-city-college

Rogerson, K. (2021, February 6). Marie Arnold writes so immigrant readers feel seen. *We Need Diverse Books Blog*. www.diversebooks.org/marie-arnold-writes-so-immigrant-readers-feel-seen

Salas Rivera, R.R. (2020). *The independence (of puerto rico)/ la independencia (de puerto rico)*. Poets.org. www.poets.org/poem/independence-puerto-rico

Salazar, A. (2020). *Land of the cranes*. Scholastic Press.

Scholastic (2020, September 29). Land of the Cranes by Aida Salazar [Video]. YouTube. www.youtube.com/watch?v=2q9ZGQuLGQ0

Seltzer, K., & de los Ríos, C. V. (2018). Translating theory to practice: Exploring teachers' raciolinguistic literacies in secondary English classrooms. *English Education, 51*(1), 49–79.

Soerens, M. (2021, July 11). DACA Was Announced Nine Years Ago. *"In the Heights" Shows Why a Better Solution is Overdue*. Immigration Resource Center of San Gabriel Valley. www.ircsgv.org/blog/2021/7/11/daca-was-announced-nine-years-ago-in-the-heights-shows-why-a-better-solution-is-overdue#:~:text=In%20the%20new%20film%20%E2%80%9CIn,U.S.%20as%20a%20small%20child

Solorzano, D., & Yosso, T. (2002). Critical race methodology: Counter-storytelling as an analytical framework for education research. *Qualitative Inquiry, 8*(1), 23–44.

Sporn, P., Gold, T., & Colón López, G. (2021). *Making the impossible possible: The story of Puerto Rican studies in Brooklyn College.* Third World Newsreel.

Suárez-Orozco, C., Súarez-Orozco, M., & Todorova, I. (2010). *Learning a new land: Immigrant students in American society.* Harvard University Press.

Sutton, R. (2022). Publishers' preview: Debut authors: Five questions for Andrea Beatriz Arango. *The Horn Book.* www.hbook.com/story/publishers-preview-debut-authors-five-questions-for-andrea-beatriz-arango

Teachers College Record (2024, May 6). The burden of acting human: Rethinking race, class, and gender experiences in U.S. independent schools - Angel Rubiel Gonzalez [Video]. The Voice. www.vimeo.com/943377134

TED (2019, June 21). My identity is a superpower - not an obstacle: America Ferrera [Video]. YouTube. www.youtube.com/watch?v=RjquHTj4HlY

The AAFCA Channel (2021, June 8). AAFCA virtual roundtable: In the Heights interview [Video]. YouTube. www.youtube.com/watch?v=hPebNSiyQtU

The Educator Collaborative (2020, April 18). Opening Session, Spring 2020 - The EdCollab Gathering [Video]. YouTube. www.youtube.com/watch?v=nz4g3YFRR7g

The Ethyle R. Wolfe Institute for the Humanities (2023, March 29). Youth literature and the Latinx diaspora [Video]. YouTube. www.youtube.com/watch?v=ZCD_bAL6u4k

The Root (2021, June 9). Let's talk about *In the Heights* and the erasure of dark-skinned Afro-Latinx folks [Video]. YouTube. www.youtube.com/watch?v=UoNYP8wlorw

The Social Life of Language. [Mike Mena] (2020, September 12). Translanguaging in 15 minutes - Otheguy, García, and Reid "Clarifying translanguaging ..." (2015) [Video]. YouTube. www.youtube.com/watch?v=Xv6cXSna4RY

The Tonight Show Jimmy Fallon. [Fallon Tonight] (2018, September 27). *Bad Bunny: Estamos bien (TV Debut)* [Video]. YouTube. www.youtube/SIQXI0UuX8M?feature=shared

Tippett, K. (Host) (2023, February 16). Ada Limón: To be made whole [Audio podcast episode]. In *On being with Krista Tippett.* www.onbeing.org/programs/ada-limon-to-be-made-whole

Tonatiuh, D. (2014). *Separate is never equal: Sylvia Mendez and her family's fight for desegregation*. Abrams.

Tse, L. (1995). Language brokering among Latino adolescents: Prevalence, attitudes, and school performance. *Hispanic Journal of Behavioral Sciences*, 17, 180–193. https://doi.org/10.1177/07399863950172003

United Nations (1989). Conventions on the Rights of the Child: General Assembly resolution 44/25. Retrieved [March 4, 2024], from www.ohchr.org/en/instruments-mechanisms/instruments/convention-rights-child

United States Courts (n.d.). *Background: Mendez v. Westminster reenactment.* United States Courts: Educational Resources. www.uscourts.gov/educational-resources/educational-activities/background-mendez-v-westminster-re-enactment

V, Alyi (Host) (2023, March 9). Lorraine Avila talks being an author and using her voice to stand up for issues in her community. [Video and Audio Podcast Episode]. In *Growing up Latina.* www.youtube.com/watch?v=zn6pP21vyfw

Vanderbilt University (2019, March 11). American Street: The American dream and the immigrant imagination with Ibi Zoboi [Video]. YouTube. www.youtube.com/watch?v=XRBHywEFzhg

Velasquez, E. (2021). *When we make it: A nuyorican novel.* Penguin Random House.

Velasquez, E. (2022). *Y si lo logramos: Una historia nuyorican.* Penguin Random House.

Vice (2020, May 20). The kids are not alright: The mental health crisis affecting Latina Teens [Video]. YouTube. www.youtube.com/watch?v=5bovfmAZZMc

Villa, L. (2021, June 10). "In the Heights" Star Gregory Diaz IV Talks Sonny, that Pool Scene, and Telling Meaningful Stories. Teen Vogue. www.teenvogue.com/story/in-the-heights-star-gregory-diaz-iv-sonny-interview

Villasante, A. (2019). *The grief keeper.* Penguin Random House.

Vogel, S., & García, O. (2017). Translanguaging. In G. Noblit & L. Moll (Eds.), *Oxford research encyclopedia of education* (pp. 1–21). Oxford University Press.

Whitney Museum of American Art (2022, November 23). No existe un mundo poshuracán: Puerto Rican art in the wake of Hurricane María [Video]. YouTube. www.youtube.com/watch?v=b2ad4VjtAF0

Woodson, J. (2001). *The other side* (E.B. Lewis, Illus.). Penguin Young Readers Group.

Workman Publishing (2021, March 30). Hear my voice [Video]. YouTube. www.youtube.com/watch?v=wS7fsjNxPfQ

Yosso, T.J. (2005). Whose culture has capital? A critical race theory discussion of community cultural wealth, *Race Ethnicity and Education*, *8*, 1, 69–91. https://doi.org.10.1080/1361332052000341006.

Zoboi, I. (2017). *American Street*. HarperCollins.

Zoboi, I. (2019). *My life as an ice cream sandwich*. Penguin Random House.

Zoboi, I. (2020). *Black enough: Stories of being young & Black in America*. HarperCollins.

Zoboi, I. (2022). *Star child: A biographical constellation of Octavia Estelle Butler*. Penguin Random House.

Zoboi, I. (2023). *Nigeria Jones*. HarperCollins.

Index